HOW TO START A VENDING MACHINE BUSINESS

Make a Full-Time Income on Autopilot with
This Step-By-Step Guide for Beginners
&
Create A Profitable Side Hustle
Saving Time and Budget

Written by

Greg Douglas

CONTENTS

ONE

STARTING A VENDING MACHINE BUSINESS: WHY AND HOW TO DO IT

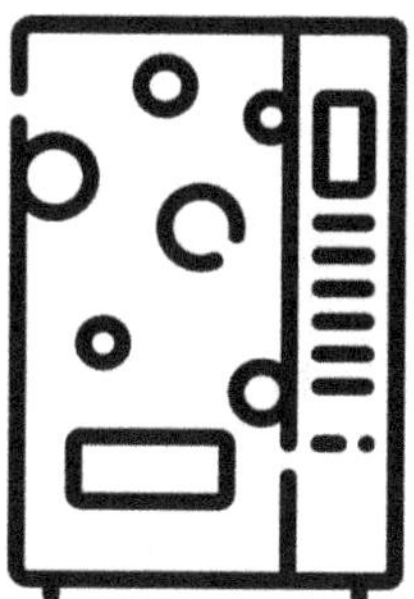

W hether it is a sudden pang outside the home or an urgent need to purchase specific items outside the canonical store hours, by now, we have become accustomed to being able to meet these needs at 24-hour automated stores, ready to provide us with everything we need.

It is enough to stroll through the streets of a city, not necessarily a metropolis, to notice that you encounter more and more vending machine stores where you can buy coffee, hot meals, souvenirs, and accessories of all kinds. If automated vending machines were once reserved for tobacco shops to meet the demands of smokers at any hour, now automated sales have expanded into other merchandise categories as well: *snacks and drinks first and foremost, but also Para-pharmacy, gadgets, adult products, and every other machinable item.*

The reasons for this success are easy to guess: h24 automated stores are always available and operating twenty-four hours a day, have become **versatile, easy to use, and above all, easy to manage**.

The sector experienced a surge thanks to the health emergency related to the Coronavirus Pandemic. The closure first and subsequent restrictions on direct-to-public sales activities encouraged the spread of H24 automated businesses.

The vending machine market is relatively small, only ranking 51st in the U.S. retail sector. However, it has some interesting numbers.

One number that indeed confirms the validity of this business is undoubtedly the **$8 billion** that the U.S. vending machine market was valued at during the pandemic period, rising to as much as $8.9 billion in 2022.

This growing number is symbolic of how much a business like this seems to continue to grow by going against the trend, despite the global crisis we are facing.

Another factor to consider is the possibility of not competing in the same sales areas as other entrepreneurs who own this business: we might even open a vending machine next to another one that is already there if we understand that there is a product that is not yet being sold that might appeal to locals.

Today, those wishing to invest in vending machines also have the opportunity to do so on a franchise basis, enjoying the benefits provided. This activity is also characterized by the *many types of contracts available* and by the formats offered. What varies, conse-quently, are the investments and the goods handled.

WHAT ARE VENDING MACHINES STORES?

24-hour vending machines are small stores, usually in premises that face central streets, strategic for pedestrian traffic, or easy to reach by car with available parking.

They can consist of as few as three vending machines; the largest can be as large as ten. They can contain and sell goods of the most varied categories: not only food and beverages (hot or fresh), but also electronic gadgets, non-prescription parapharmacy products such as patches or condoms, and adult items, which have proven to be attractive products for the market, as the vending store provides maximum privacy at the time of purchase.

In short, h24 automatic stores vary in size and content, but they have in common that they offer a service that is *always open, easy to reach, and requires little financial and labor management and maintenance*. While h24 automatic shops meet the needs of consumers, they are also depopulating because they are an attractive investment for entrepreneurs. This attracts even the small ones and those who want to test themselves in the commercial sector, since they provide an ongoing income for little initial capital and so little work and management commitment that they make them the perfect side business to take care of in the free time left over from the primary work employment.

In addition, 24-hour automated stores are widely **adaptable and versatile**. For example, they can be inside premises facing the street, such as traditional snack & drink outlets open twenty-four hours a day or outdoor kiosks on the sidewalk. Finally, they can also be an addition to an existing physical store, thus enabling the business to increase its service hours.

Fun fact: the first type of vending machine was invented 2,000 years ago in Greece by Heron of Alexandria, capable of dispensing holy water to be used in rituals in Egyptian temples.

WHY OPEN AN AUTOMATIC STORE OR SELF-SERVICE BAR?

Of all successful small businesses, certainly, the 24-hour self-service café and store are among those that offer the greatest profitability while offering flexibility in terms of working hours.

The main features that make these businesses truly unique follow:

- *Absence of staff*: the staff within this business is practically nonexistent. The manager has to limit himself to stocking the dispensers on time and ensuring their proper functioning;
- *Small premises*: a small studio apartment is enough to be able to open a self-service bar or vending machine store;
- *Freedom to run the business*: for those deciding to open their own business, this is definitely something that could make a difference. Machine replenishment and maintenance do not require much effort, so you can fully manage your time!
- *No specific skills are required*: anyone can open this type of business. Just choose the suitable suppliers and attend the different training courses that they activate for their clients;
- *Low initial investment*: One of this activity's advantages is undoubtedly the initial investment. In fact, with about 10 thousand dollars, it is possible to start a small business quietly;
- *High profitability*: the good margins on products, the absence of staff costs, and the business opening can only make these activities very profitable.

THINGS TO KNOW BEFORE OPENING AN AUTOMATIC STORE

Let us now see what the indispensable elements of such a business are.

A 24-hour self-service business includes vending machines, a **machine to change bills into "change,"** and in some cases a few shelves and a **microwave oven** to entice more people to buy meals to reheat.

The **size of the room is**, of course, a function of the number of vending machines present. More vending machines means more varied offerings and thus more appeal.

In addition, many suppliers offer better terms to those who own multiple distributors, allowing higher profit margins. One must, therefore, first identify the right venue and then study everything else.

WHERE CAN VENDING MACHINES BE INSTALLED?

If you want to make money, you have to choose the correct location.

The right locations are in areas with high foot traffic, such as malls, schools, airports, train stations, large office complexes, nearby stores, and so on.

There must be no other distributors. Often the ideal locations are already equipped with vending machines, and vendors have exclusive selling rights.

The right location alone is not enough.

In order to start making money as soon as possible, you have to **sell the right product in the right place.**

To better understand this concept, a candy machine is unlikely to be successful if placed near a health food store!

You have to study the target audience relative to the area you choose. Remember that if you opt for franchising, the parent company may rule out selling a given product, despite high traffic, because it is out of the target market.

Generally, dispensers are always placed at the *entrance to an office or in a highly visible place*, in many cases, it can become an actual furniture component.

Indeed, the "crowded" and high-transit places give those who operate one or more vending machines the greatest satisfaction. In particular, where younger people are concentrated, we see the most sustained sales: *schools and universities, hostels, gyms, and communities. Gas stations, airports, and stations are other recommended locations.*

Recent studies show how, in areas frequented by blue-collar workers, average spending on vending machines has more than doubled. Consider this finding when deciding where to place your business.

In order to have a clearer idea of where to proceed with the installation, it is helpful to conduct a **preliminary analysis of the area**, considering the type of products you plan to sell.

In addition, it is important to inquire about your county's current permits before you can dispense certain services and products, such as in the case of cigarettes or alcohol. Still, we will explore this further in the following chapters.

A LIST OF BEST LOCATIONS FOR YOUR BUSINESS

As we have already mentioned, the location is the key to your business: if any passersby do not see it, you will not sell enough.

There are also some aspects to bear in mind, such as the *impossibility of installing a machine on someone else's property* since you will not be able to use its water connections or electricity. To do this, you will need a contract with the landlord, where you will have to agree on the type of payment based on the consumption of your business.

This may also prove to be a complicated process, having to deal with an **outsider who may demand a share of the earnings**.

Once you set everything up, you can start your business.

Let's see what might be the best places to do this:

1. *Industrial parks*: logistics and distribution centers are often located in the suburbs, far from bars and restaurants, and frequented all day long by workers who, tired from the day, may require quick refreshments, choosing your business. Here your main competitors may be food trucks serving food during breaks.

2. *Parks*: When people leave the office during a lunch break and go to the park to consume food, due to the rush, they might need to buy a drink, indulge in a dessert, or drink a hot coffee to recharge their batteries.

3. *Residential buildings*: In these buildings, which function similarly to a motel, people are used to consuming from vending machines and buying products such as tobacco, magazines, or even cosmetics.

4. *Hospitals*: with a constant coming and going, vending machines in hospitals can please both the relatives of the sick person and the sick person himself, who may want to indulge in a treat during a stressful time such as an illness. In this case, you have to think about what a patient who, in a hurry, has forgotten something at home might really need: a charger or headphones to watch a movie in peace during their hospital stay might turn out to be a real bargain for you!

5. *Hotels and Motels*: what do you think costs more between ordering room service or going to the vending machines? Hotels are a strategic spot for vending machines because of constant foot traffic.

6. *Parking lots*: when we come back from a long walk and want to find refreshment before driving off again, vending machines can be an excellent solution for many people, and this also applies to underground parking lots.

7. *Gyms*: what could be better than a snack after a tiring workout session? Areas near gyms are really strategic spots for your business if you know how to keep your customers happy: protein snacks, sports drinks, and supplements can quickly be sold to people who are trying to improve their bodies. Also, if you are about to work out and forget your water or towel at home, vending machines can prove to be a quick and convenient solution to your problem!

8. *Study places*: When there is no cafeteria at the place of study or academic dormitory to feed students, vending machines can prove to be a really profitable business. In these cases, however, there is the affordability of students, which is lower than that of workers, to consider. For this reason, selling products that are cheaper and sustainable from a kid's pocket is recommended.

9. *Laundromat*: Why not treat yourself to a snack while you wait for your laundry to be done? Laundromats are popular

places, keeping in mind that not every American family can afford a washing machine.

With your vending machines, you can offer both products to fill your stomach and products to better wash your dirty laundry, such as detergent or fabric softener.

THE PROS AND CONS OF VENDING MACHINES STORES

Automated 24-hour stores meet the needs of the hectic life of our cities, responding to a civilization that increasingly needs immediate availability. Moreover, as we have already seen, they are spreading because they represent an attractive economic opportunity, advantageous without the significant risks of a large investment.

In fact, opening a small automatic store does not require a long previous experience in the commercial sector: it is an excellent initiative to test one's entrepreneurial initiative precisely because **the starting capital is minimal** compared to any other commercial area. If you want to open a successful automated store, it is crucial to *find a good location to rent in a pedestrian transit hub of the city* or with a parking lot in an area where cars pass through. Once you find the perfect location, you must fill it with the most suitable vending machines.

Now, let's see what the pros of opening a business like this are:

1. The first thing to do is to <u>buy or rent a vending machine</u>, having enough cash to fill each machine with products. This will be the only action that needs to be done regularly, along with cleaning the environment, and you will not even need to hire waiters or cooks: the machine will do all the work for you!

2. The <u>expenses to carry on the business are very low</u>, or at least lower than any business that requires staff, having only to pay the location rent and taxes.

3. You can <u>receive payments from cashless people</u>, thanks to

contactless technology that allows customers to pay using their smartphones, smartwatches, or any other device connected to a card. This will allow you not to have too much cash to withdraw at the end of the day, avoiding the risks associated with collecting and carrying cash. In addition, vending machines have this payment technology automatically integrated into them, so you won't have to worry about looking for a dedicated provider for this service.

4. Your <u>revenues are not limited to certain hours of the day</u>, unlike traditional retail stores that have hours when consumers can buy products.

5. Your vending machines will be <u>operating every day of the week</u>, at any hour. All you have to ensure is that the machines have product inside and that the environment is clean.

6. You will also <u>take advantage of unconventional times</u>, such as work break times, in this way, by going out to target people who perhaps like to go out at night, stay late at night, and enjoy a late-night snack. Also, on days such as Sundays or holidays when all the other stores will not be working, your machines will be there working for you!

7. <u>You will not have to do a lot of maintenance work</u>. Vending machines are a mostly passive activity because once you have created the environment and have installed the machines, your only job will be to restock and clean up. The only kind of inconvenience regarding vending machines will be having to repair any malfunctions or, in the case of vandalism, replace damaged parts. Not counting these kinds of eventualities, the only work you will have to do is to decide how often to withdraw money from the machines (once a week might be more than enough) and bring home your cash.

8. <u>There is no product that you cannot sell</u>. As we have already said, when deciding what to sell with your vending machine, you have to deal with the area of your machines.

Coffee machines will sell more near universities and offices, condom machines and adult items will sell better near motels, and so on.

Now that I have incited your desire to open a business like this, it is time to list all the cons you will face.

It is likely that by spending more, you will earn more. This means that your business is unlikely to profit from just one machine. If you want to leave your 9-to-5 business and survive on the profits generated by your business, you will have to plan to scale your business and slowly add more machines. On average, a distributor located in a reasonably profitable area can bring you home **$300 a month**. If you're planning to place distributors in an area you're not sure about, profits may even be lower. Therefore, when you plan to start such a business, I recommend that you think early on about how to expand by setting up more outlets to earn much more money and get rid of your current job.

You will find competition in the best locations. When you think you have found a profitable location, be prepared to compete with other business owners who decide to place their machines in the same place.

1. *Small additional expenses can weigh.* When you create your business plan, you need to calculate rent, licenses, permits, electricity and insurance in your budget. These will be your fixed expenses, so consider the income you aim to make concerning these expenses.

2. *Vandalism is a risk for you.* As seen in the pros, there may be people in some areas who want to cause damage to your business. Take this kind of damage into account because it could weigh on your income.

3. The cost of these machines is also calculated on the basis of everything related to a possible after-sales service. In fact, *spare parts are of considerable importance in this business.* So, choosing a supplier company that cannot quickly obtain the parts needed in case of failure can be a serious problem.

A nonfunctioning distributor translates into a loss in economic terms. Same goes for suppliers of products for sale!

4. It may happen that for the most disparate reasons, you may have to *suffer restrictive measures on opening hours*.
   Therefore, it is good to consider this eventuality and assess the sustainability of the business in case of such problems.

That is why, before opening, it is necessary to carry out good planning, as with any business idea. The business plan is that document in which you indicate all aspects of your future business (costs, desirable profits, problems to be faced, growth margin, etc.).

Your business plan should be as realistic as possible. However, in the specifics of vending cannot miss market research to test the feasibility of your idea.

For example, by checking the location of existing vending machines and talking to business owners, you can find out what to focus on and whether the market is already saturated.

Another factor you should consider when choosing a location is the rate of theft and crime. Best to avoid areas with high rates of theft and vandalism.

Theft and car damage quickly bring down the rate of profits.

Better to choose highly visible areas that are frequently monitored by law enforcement or security cameras.

Don't rule out installing a surveillance system if you want to feel safer and your targeted area needs it.

TWO
SCANNING OF COSTS

HOW MUCH DOES IT COST TO OPEN A VENDING MACHINE BUSINESS?

Vending machines are increasingly entering people's daily lives, and the hectic life of recent times continually increases the demand for them.

Everywhere we go (to the office, school, hospital), we only have to look around to find at least one vending machine. But, of course, this is not a random occurrence, but **a response to an end-consumer need.**

This has been exacerbated in recent years to the point that it has become an American as well as a European phenomenon, with 24-

hour self-service stores located in studio apartments where the vending offerings range from drinks to condoms.

Focusing on coffee vending machines and hot beverage vending machines in general, those wishing to get started should expect *a minimum investment of about 3,000 to 7,000 dollars.* Typically, a small model costs between 200 and 500 dollars. *A medium-sized dispenser goes up in the range of 1,200 to 3,000 dollars.*

The largest ones, in some cases, can require as much as 5,000 dollars. Still, this is not too high a cost, especially compared to customized machines. In fact, in that case, the expense tends to range between 10,000, to 200,000-300,000 dollars.

These costs also depend on the volume of the order, how large the vending machines are, the components, the details of the machines you want to have, and how complex it is to complete the order.

Usually, it is possible to find customization of the vending machines that sell snacks and beverages for zero price since the basic design is easily replicable. Still, for more specific devices, with shapes and sizes on customers' request, much more expense is usually required.

There are also *combined dispensers, super-accessorized* and equipped with a *touch-screen interface,* the cost of which can reach more than *30,000 dollars.*

You could easily access financing from the bank for medium to small projects that do not require large amounts of start-up capital, which is why it is essential to have a business plan to present.

Partnering with those with capital to invest could be another good way to find the resources you need to get started.

FRANCHISING VENDING MACHINES: CAN THEY BE TRUSTED?

Relying on a Franchise can have both negative and positive aspects, and now we are going to examine them together.

Affiliating with a vending machine franchise is a winning choice for numerous reasons.

First and foremost, you have a wide range of offerings to choose from.

It frequently happens that it is the vending machine companies themselves who have come up with franchises.

In addition, you would avoid taking unnecessary risks and face less workload by facing low start-up costs.

In particular, based on the experience already gained, **the parent company can guide you in choosing the right location**, approaching the machines and replenishing products.

Finally, you would have a way to train and be supported all along the way in starting your business.

As you can see, opening a vending machine business is a business with few barriers to entry. However, by working hard and putting the tips into practice, you can create a stable income that you can count on even in times of economic uncertainty.

There are also cases where a franchise is not the solution we expect it to be.

Cases have happened of entrepreneurs who had bad experiences with some of the industry's most "emblazoned" companies. Apparently, *many companies*, which make turnkey vending machine stores, *have allegedly failed to keep their promises to their customers*. The most common sin seems to be that they either disappear after starting the store or charge "astronomical" service and maintenance costs!

Given the existence of this possibility, we advise you always to try to inform yourself to the best of your ability before proceeding.

WHAT TYPE TO CHOOSE

If you wish to enter this world, you can consider several options:

- *Affiliation with a vending machine franchise* is the recommended mode. You will be able to take advantage of an established business model based on selling a given product in a specific area, avoiding taking unnecessary risks.

- *By purchasing vending machines yourself,* you will have maximum freedom of choice. You will be free to buy just a few vending machines and then expand later if opportunities and finances permit. But, at the same time, you will face high risks. In addition, you must work hard: both to procure and purchase machines and to find the right stations.
- *Buying used vending machines* gives you the advantage of having immediate cash flow from your existing business. But you have to be careful, understanding well why the old owner wants to get rid of the business. Then, it's up to you to do some thorough research on the existing business, including checking accounts, inspecting machines, reviewing existing contracts, and evaluating positions.

When deciding what kind of vending machine to buy, we need to consider our target audience and the profits we aim to make.

This is why there are different types of vending machines, which we will now analyze together.

The first type is the one that, concerning expenses, guarantees the highest earnings. Still, these are pocket change when compared with real vending machines: we are talking about **vending machines for bulk products**, such as those for chewing gum, stickers, or small toys, which mainly have two significant advantages:

1. The product inside, bought in bulk, has *ridiculous costs*, and the customer perceives the purchase as convenient since, for less than a dollar, he gets a large amount of product, which will cost you very few cents.
2. The vending machine *has no costs related to the power supply* and, consequently, maintenance of the electrical part, which could spoil over time, becoming a real passive business that you will only have to supply with the product. The only kind of maintenance you will have to do will be related to the mechanical part's

possible failures, which are less rare than the electrical type failures that ordinary vending machines might have.

These vending machines cost no more than $450, and starting as low as $150 they can be an excellent bargain for your business.

The second type, the most common, is the *vending machines that dispense drinks and snacks*. Again, we have already seen what the prices are. Still, if we set out to look for used vending machines, we may even be able, with prices ranging from $1,000 to $3,000, to get an excellent device in excellent condition and, in this case, the revenue per product can go over a net dollar.

The third type, the customized vending machines, can be a double-edged sword. If you have conducted the best market study, a custom vending machine to sell the product you know will be in demand will be successful. Still, it requires a much higher expense to create than buying a standard vending machine.

In these cases, **finding a used custom vending machine that will do the trick is very rare**, so you will likely be forced to start with a much higher budget.

Having learned this information, it will be up to you to analyze where you want to pursue your business, understanding whether your target audience will be willing to spend little. Therefore you should favor selling bulk products, whether they will want something more expensive, opting for product customization, or whether they only want a quick snack, opting for classic vending machines.

ADVANTAGES AND DISADVANTAGES OF USED VENDING MACHINES

Trying to save money at the beginning of your business is a move that could prove successful. In an industry like the vending machine business, saving on the very core of the business can lead to spending even half the budget we had in mind to start, or at least that is what it may seem like.

Remember that we never know what kind of damage used vending machines have suffered, so they may malfunction over time much sooner than a new machine would.

Also, it is not true for all vending machines that replacement parts are always available: with older models you may not be able to get more service from the manufacturer, completely negating the initial savings and forcing you to spend the money on a new devices. Let's also consider that **the spare parts of older devices**, when available, **turn out to be much more expensive than the current ones**. Therefore, it is understandable why it is necessary to get the best information before buying a used machine.

Also, consider that the longer your vending machine remains broken, the more losses your business will have to suffer. For this reason, if your goal is to save money, I recommend that you do not buy used but refurbished vending machines, as the latter, before being sold, go under the control of experienced companies that repair them and ensure their proper functioning.

Therefore, buy a used vending machine only if you are sure that you know its working condition.

The place from which you buy the vending machine also influences the ease of repair if it is damaged: if the headquarters of the company that sells you the device is many miles away from that of your business, consider the time and possible cost it will take to get replacement parts in or ship the machine as far as needed.

Finally, also consider that used vending machines often have one major flaw: because they are dated, they run only on cash.

In a time like this, in which contactless and direct payment systems from one's smartphone are depopulating, not allowing your customer to pay when they have forgotten their wallet at home or are short on change will result in a loss of your earnings.

However, suppose you perform a study of the market you want to invest in and find that your audience is not interested in paying with the more technological methods. In that case, *you can also opt for a reconditioned machine in good condition.*

Two sites you can use to search for vending machines suitable for your business are Vending.com and onlinevending.com.

On sites like Naturals2Go.com and evending.com, you will find reasonably priced vending machines, both used and new, and you can also receive financing for your device.

If one of your vending machines fails, you can find them on a site I recommend. discountvending.com. sells parts and accessories that might fit your vending machine.

THE LATEST GENERATION OF VENDING MACHINES

For many people *interfacing with something technological can be an extra push to buy from your vending machines* if they feature a touch screen. Now imagine the effect of more advanced systems such as fingerprint or voice stamp recognition.

An example of a vending machine that has the unbelievable is those from *MinuteKey*: these are machines in which, once you insert your key, you can receive an exact copy of it in just one minute!

What would be so extraordinary, you ask?

Once you have made the first copy, the machine allows you to register your fingerprint: that way, if you lose all your keys, you can go to any MinuteKey device and request a new key simply using your fingerprint!

Many customers appreciate those who offer them the greatest possible convenience.

So let's repeat what features of a MinuteKey machine should not be missed:

1. *Touch screen*: makes it easier to navigate between products and makes the experience more convenient.
2. *Contactless or card payment*: when someone pays by card or smartphone, the money will come directly to your bank account as a transfer. If you rent the device, you may have to pay fees to the owner.
3. *Refunds*: if customers fail to collect their product, a quick refund may happen only through the latest machines. You should not underestimate this aspect, as some customers

may react badly when the vending machine does not give change or the product itself, starting to hit it and causing you a taste to have to repair. That is why a more high-tech vending machine, despite costing more, could save you hundreds of dollars!

4. *You will always know how sales are going*: the new vending machine sales monitoring systems are accurate and reliable. This way, while you are at home, you can check which products are selling best, knowing which and how many to bring from your warehouse to replenish the vending machines.

My advice is as follows: if your warehouse and residence are in close proximity to the vending machines, you can install less high-tech devices without too many problems, while if you need to control your business remotely, technology will come to your rescue, avoiding many problems and ensuring optimal operation.

THREE
HOW MUCH DO YOU MAKE PER MONTH FROM VENDING MACHINES?

The answer is by no means easy. Much (indeed everything) depends on the location and the products for sale chosen. You have to have some marketing savvy and understand what the local or transient population may need in that particular place. For example, **finding a place near an office where there is a lack of a bar is a good investment**. But several similar insights can make a difference in earnings.

As we have already seen, opening a vending machine requires an initial investment. Therefore, among the elements to consider before opening such a business is to consider one's budget. Once you understand the amount you want to allocate for this investment, you can start looking for the necessary machinery and the premises in which to place it.

The first important search is for the venue. Finding the right venue can intercept a specific type of clientele and thus facilitate earnings.

You have to consider one key factor when starting a business like this: there is not much advertising that can be done to vending machines, especially online, and you must focus instead on their usefulness. The right vending machine in the right place will make a difference and lead to profits.

Initial costs alone certainly can change considerably depending on the type of distributor we choose.

In fact, it only takes a brief online search to unearth a rather large number of types of distributors, starting from new, used, old, large or smaller, traditional, or selling more extravagant items. Then, local, distributors and finally objects, this is the last point to put the investment to good use. In fact, it may be a good idea to sell objects or food products, depending on the location where the business will arise.

There is also a final option: *franchising*. This type of investment allows you to save on some expenses, such as distributors, but it has an operating cost that is usually equivalent to 20 percent of revenues.

You should also consider maintenance in the initial expenses. You could find it included in the contract in the case of a franchise.

But then, how much do you make from vending machines?

Drawing up the plan, *you can't miss the figure on earnings when figuring out whether to invest or not.* Here these are pure examples since it all depends on how many products you manage to sell and the percentage you get from their sale, thus excluding the expense of buying the products.

Taking an example of all possible expenses, one can say that earnings should be around $40,000 annually if one can sell an equivalent of $100 to $110 worth of products per day. At this point, you have to subtract the cost of renting the premises (if you do not own it), worth about $500 per month, and the percentage of the franchise (if you have entered into a contract). In total, you end up making about $26,000, from which you remove the expense of electricity and taxes. Is it a bargain? It's up to you.

WHAT TO SELL WITH YOUR VENDING MACHINES

One of the strengths of this business is that it can be adapted to sell any kind of food, from frozen to baked. All you need is the right vending machine.

Among the most popular ones are:

- *Coffee, tea and hot chocolate* vending machines sell well just about everywhere especially near offices, universities and shopping centers.
- The same applies if you choose to install a vending machine for *cold drinks and snacks* such as chips and chocolate bars.
- Food and beverage vending machines such as *hot sandwiches and sandwiches* work best in corporate and student environments.
- *Sweets and toys suit* shopping malls, supermarkets, and playgrounds where there is a high attendance of families.
- *Personal hygiene products* such as detergents, toothpaste, and over-the-counter medications do best when sold at gas stations and public service facilities.

To maximize profits, you must set out to find suppliers, preferably wholesalers, who can offer you the best price for each item.

HOW TO FURNISH YOUR VENDING MACHINES

We finally have the place of our dreams, now it needs to be fixed up in the best possible way. Among the necessary works, one of the most important for a 24h automatic store is the work on the electrical system: for example, it would be good if each vending machine had its own individual circuit breaker, that way, if a short circuit were to occur on a device, only this one would stop working, while the rest of the automatic store would continue its activity.

It would help if you did not underestimate the design area: it is essential to create an environment that is pleasant, welcoming, and intuitive. Remember that people are often distracted and always in a hurry. Hence, factors such as lighting, visual cues, materials, and accessibility are crucial in giving a good user experience and ensuring that your customers will soon return to shop at our automated store.

THE 5 TIPS FOR INCREASING EARNINGS MARGINS BY MORE THAN 30%

Following these five tips will allow your business to always run at 100 percent of its potential, so you always get the most out of it.

1. Machines should always be well stocked, so plan visits according to your needs.
2. *Cleanliness is the watchword.* A dirty vending machine is unlikely to attract attention in a positive sense from customers.
3. Repairs must be *addressed in a timely manner.*
4. *Customer service must be impeccable.* Providing contact information such as an email or phone number to call, a whatsapp or Telegram contact that is clearly visible is helpful for the customer to report malfunctions and problems.
5. Make sure that you always sell *products that have an earlier expiration date first.*
6. *Periodically analyze sales* to understand what appeals most to the customer and what just doesn't have appeal.

It is essential to emphasize how crucial the fifth point is: **a product**

that doesn't sell is taking up space in your vending machines, while one that sells out quickly leaves customers coming into your establishment dissatisfied, for example, because of the absence of their favorite candy bar.

DIFFERENCE BETWEEN TAXABLE AND NONTAXABLE PRODUCTS

Sales tax concerning vending machines follows special rules you should know before starting.

As far as food is concerned, the only taxable items sold through vending machines are convenience foods, soft drinks, candy, and dietary supplements.

Machines that require the use of a coin for activation or electronic payment are taxable, including activities like batting cages, cranes, foosball and pool tables, fortune-telling machines, jukeboxes, photo or video booths, rides, video, and pinball games.

The sale of personal hygiene or beauty products is of interest, as some are not taxable.

Taxable ones include antiperspirants, baby lotions, combs, condoms, cosmetics, hand lotions, shampoo, soap, sunscreen, toothbrushes, and toothpaste.

On the other hand, products that do not require taxation are baby bottles, diapers, feminine hygiene products, pacifiers, and teething rings.

This may make us think about dedicating a space in our business to baby services, thus looking for an area with a high birth rate and a large number of babies.

In this way, when a mother due to distraction has run out of her diapers in the middle of the night and does not know how to change her baby, she can access them through your vending machines, finding your business indispensable and becoming a loyal buyer!

In any case, always find out beforehand what kind of laws and divitets are in force in the place where you are operating so that you do not sell products that are considered illegal by your state's legislation. If you were to sell an illegal product, *you would risk a fine from the authorities, leading, in the worst case, to a closure.*

In addition, industry competition laws prevent you from selling certain types of products in close proximity to direct competitors.

FOUR

THE PERFECT SPOT

HOW TO CHOOSE WHERE TO PLACE YOUR BUSINESS

When you are deciding where in the city to install our new business, there are factors to consider that might be good indicators of how profitable the area is.

Indeed, deciding to install the machines in areas with a lot of foot traffic is a good idea. **These areas include schools and offices, very busy places with the constant movement of people.**

When we realize that there is a traffic of people who might pass by a particular spot, we might decide to survey it, frequenting the area for several days.

I advise observing how foot traffic behaves on weekdays and weekends, as the trend of people coming and going could change based on work activity.

During your survey days, you will need to count the number of pedestrians who, during their walk, will pass by your business.

If the number is around 25 to 30 passersby, then you can consider the area as average to good.

An area with average traffic ranging from 70 passersby and up is considered highly profitable, since of those 70 it is likely that each day at least 7 people will spend an average of $2 to $5 in your machines, for a profit that can range from $100 to $300 weekly, and $400 to $1,000 monthly.

These numbers are indicative, as it is likely that foot traffic will also go over **300 to 400 daily passersby in highly frequented areas on weekends**, providing you with truly substantial earnings.

As we have discussed in previous chapters, areas highly frequented by blue-collar, service-sector workers have a very high spending rate on vending machines. This, according to Barry Strickland, a former owner of more than 250 vending machines scattered throughout San Diego, is since white-collar workers are inclined to spend more to get more upscale meals, not settling for the quick and often unhealthy product like the classic packaged sweet or sandwich snack that can be found in vending machines.

When deciding where to locate our business then, we need to consider what businesses are in the area: any type of business that involves manual and heavy labor will have a higher percentage of people interested in buying goods from the vending machines.

Suppose you were considering opening an upscale vending machines business that sells high-ticket products like caviar and placing it near significant offices. In that case, *I recommend that you do extensive research before proceeding.*

Among the factors to consider as you search for your perfect spot are:

1. *The cost of rent.* As much as expensive places have high

consumer demand, the cost of renting can be a significant burden for those who are starting this business. However, you can get around the rental cost problem by finding a venue that is not too large, so you can save money and still work at total capacity with the machines.

2. *High-end consumers.* When you're deciding what kind of consumers you want to attract, consider that there are ways to attract wealthy consumers even with a business like this: premium-looking, high-ticket product customized vending machines could convince even the most affluent consumer to buy from you, although, as mentioned earlier, the tendency to spend money in this way is much lower in wealthy white-collar workers. Two representative examples of this trend are Moët et Chandon and Kratom Crazy Sprinkles, with their premium-grade machines that are sure to convince even the most discerning customer.

3. *Area businesses.* Among your main competitors, you will find not only the other entrepreneurs who will decide to start vending machine businesses near yours because of the profitability of the location, but also other types of businesses that might sell the same products as you, but owning staff and offering a "warmer" service to the consumer. Don't be too frightened by this aspect: many consumers prefer not to have direct contact with a bar or restaurant staff, preferring the intimacy and privacy of a vending machine. One such example is one of Europe's most famous capitals, Amsterdam.

4. Full of activities that can satisfy the appetites of tourists from all over the world who come there to spend days of fun, Amsterdam was able to answer a very particular demand of such a place: many people do not feel like communicating when they are in an altered state, so they prefer to eat junk food without having the slightest human contact. That's where "FEBO" comes in, *automated machines that serve burgers and tater tots at all hours of the*

day, pleasing the palates of those who, after having had a busy day, want to enjoy a warm and delicious bite.This type of business differs slightly from the traditional vending machine business. However, it is part of it since staff is required to prepare the food. Still, it fully embodies one of the reasons why people may prefer vending machines to ordinary restaurants: **the total absence of contact with other people and the desire to eat something good very quickly**. If you think you know an area with a high concentration of people looking for hot meals and who would prefer not to have to deal with servers, then this business style might be for you.

5. *Competition.* Sometimes a location is not suitable because there are too many direct competitors. Direct competitors are companies that sell similar products or services and hope to attract a similar target market. The only competitive advantage is to operate near indirect competitors. These companies operate in the same industry but sell different products or services and serve other target markets. The presence of indirect competitors can increase sales because you can attract twice as many customers. An example of indirect competition that might help you find the right kind of product for your business: yoga is an indirect competitor to aspirin since these medicines promise to make headaches go away, but so does yoga. To find the central problem your target audience has, look for an alternative product to what you already offer to fill the gap.

6. Another factor to consider is the distance between suppliers and your machine location. The farther your machine is, the more expensive it will be to procure and transport products. In addition, if you plan to hire employees to operate your device (even though it will not be necessary), you will also need to consider how far your machine is from public transportation systems.

As seen in the example of "FEBO," in some cases, you may need full-time employees, but generally, you will only need to find someone to take care of cleaning the rooms and supplying the vending machines.

Initially, you may decide to take care of this yourself to save costs, but over time, if you get to run more than one store, you will be forced to hire staff.

The distance from your warehouse to the store is a factor to consider: travel will also have costs, and you will need to consider what these will be for the workers you hire to take care of your asset.

Fun fact: the need to have no contact with the seller for the customer is first exploited by Richard Carlile, a British publisher who thought of selling risqué newspapers through automated vendors, so as to eliminate the shame of buyers who wished to purchase one.

WHEN TO RELY ON A TRACKING SERVICE

If you are unclear about where to position your business to make the most profit, one of the ways to remedy the problem is to rely on a location-based service.

Researchgate is an excellent example of a service that can provide you with good pointers for implementing your business.

The companies you should turn to are undoubtedly those that get to talk to the owners or managers of the places you are interested in instead of you, saving you the trouble and time of talking to each of them personally.

Obviously, we are talking about a service that has a certain kind of cost to be added to those to be incurred for a possible renovation of the venue, installing the machines, supplying them, and so on.

A DEAL THAT COULD PROVE TO BE A LUCRATIVE ONE

What I'm about to tell you is a tip that, should you succeed in putting it into practice, could really change the fortunes of your business: **when a mall is in the midst of its construction, it's a good idea to try to contact the prospective owners to pitch your business inside**, so that you can grab a good slice of the earnings first.

In addition, if you show that you care about your machines by performing constant maintenance, offering a good product, and bringing a good slice of earnings to the mall, you will likely be able to expand the number of premises inside!

Let me remind you that, on average, 25-30 daily passersby is already a good number for a business like this. Let's think about the turnout of a mall and the usefulness of a beverage and snack vending machine throughout the day. You can already imagine what kind of business we are talking about: a golden opportunity!

THE RIGHT PRODUCT IN THE RIGHT PLACE

We have already talked about how crucial it is to study the habits of the average consumer who frequents the area of your business, but let's now look at what are the three primary and representative categories of the vending machine business.

The first is definitely **snack and soda machines**, the most popular ones throughout America and probably the world, since they are easily refillable, have **really low maintenance costs** and can quickly meet the demand of many customers. Naturally, those who start this kind of business usually try this kind of machine, since it guarantees almost sure earnings, but, on the other hand, it forces us to have to compete with a great many others who, like us, have decided to opt for this kind of machine.

As for ways to top up these machines, do not stop solely at simple sneakers and sugary drinks, as it may happen that those who are dieting and looking for something tasty and that is not too fatty want to opt for healthy food.

Now let's see what the foods and drinks that Americans prefer to find in vending machines are:

- Let's start with *bars*, the most popular product among Americans up to 10 years ago, according to NBC news.
- *Pop Tars*, with *Frosted Strawberry* and *Brown Sugar Cinnamon* flavors, are among Americans' favorite breakfast substitutes.
- *Chips*, with their ease of consumption and unquestionably good flavor, are great for satiating hunger or accompanying one's meal. I recommend Sun Chips because of their low-fat content, but there are many lovers of the classic and timeless *Lays* out there, so don't rule them out.
- •One of the most beloved foods of the baby boomer generation, *Peanut Butter Risis* can be found in so many vending machines, and why they are so popular is undoubtedly no mystery. As many as 81 percent of those surveyed by YouGov said they love them! *Clif bars*, a viable alternative to higher-calorie bars, are suitable for those seeking a burst of energy, such as a worker who has been lifting heavy loads in the sun since morning.
- *Planter trail mixes* can be a handy tool in your machine: peanuts, chocolate, and raisins, sweet and savory, all in one snack. This can win over lovers of contrasting flavors.
- With their excellent nutrients, *Granola bars* are the choice for those who want a snack throughout the day. *Nature's Valley, Kind bars*, and *Chewy granola bars* are the most prominent.
- Crackers, a quick, healthy, and tasty snack, are the choice of a great many when they have to spend the day away from home. *Cheez-its* are not very beneficial, but they are a favorite among Americans. You can also opt for other types of less fatty and salty crackers, so they can please everyone.
- *Chex mixes* are a delicious variety of different kinds of salty snacks, adored by those who prefer salty to sweet, that pack

many different types of salty snacks in one bag. Including them in your vending machine could prove to be a winning choice.

- You can't go wrong by adding pretzels to your vending machine. *Pretzels* are popular snacks because they are relatively healthy, low-fat, and low-calorie. In addition, pretzels appeal to so many Americans because of the energy they give you with their complex carbohydrates. *Rold Gold*, Snyder's, and *Goldfish Pretzels* are three of the favorite brands.

But when starting this kind of business, it is good not to stop at just simple snacks: we have already talked about specific products that could attract clientele and may even deviate a lot from classic machine foods. Now, let's look at some of them together.

- *Frozen desserts* attract many clients who prefer ice cream to simple bars. This type of machine requires a more significant amount of energy to operate, having to maintain shallow temperatures. Some of the best-known and most reliable brands of vending machines include *Frozen Treat's Ice Cream.*
- *Coin-operated laundromats*, with washing products, are good business in large cities.
- *Cigarette vending machines*, selling an indispensable product for smokers even at night, are among the most profitable vending machines. Of course, you will need specific state permits to sell cigarettes, so find out about them before proceeding.
- *Pizza machines*, capable of serving customers a pizza in a matter of minutes, are the salvation for those who, in the middle of the night, would like to bite into a piece of pizza with stringy mozzarella cheese but cannot do so because of the time of day. There are two types of these machines: the former work by reheating frozen pizzas, offering a cheaper

product to the consumer, while the latter can prepare pizzas by rolling out the dough, pouring sauce and coating the surface with mozzarella cheese, and then baking the pizza in an electric oven.

For both types of machines, the costs become much lower by the time demand for the product is very high and continues over time, as the oven temperature to get to baking will already be high enough to cook the next pizza.

Fun fact: The first type of cigarette vending machine dates back to the 17th century and was installed in many English bars, selling tobacco products, while the first vending machine installed in America, which later became wildly popular, was the Thomas Adams Gum Company's tutti-frutti chewing gum machine in 1888, which later expanded the business by installing different types of vending machines with other products inside them.

HOW TO MAKE MORE MONEY WITH PRODUCTS IN YOUR VENDING MACHINES

When deciding what kind of product to put in our vending machines, we have to come to terms with the earnings each individual product will have to bring us. Therefore, as much as there are products that we would like to put inside the vending machines, if we cannot get them through a source that is economical for us, it will be a problem to be able to earn enough to cover the costs of energy, rent and the product itself.

Therefore, among the essentials of starting a business like this, one of the main points is definitely to get in touch with a supplier who can sell us the product at moderate prices. Of course, wholesale markets come to our aid in such cases.

Samsclub is an excellent site to get you snickers bars and candy of various kinds to put in your vending machines.

The low prices will allow you to keep the costs in the vending machines competitive and in line with the rest of the businesses that will be selling the same product as you nearby.

Https://www.samsclub.com/?Xid=hdr_logo

Among the most popular suppliers, we find "Healthy Snack Solutions" suitable if you are looking to stock your vending machines with healthy and cheap items. As we have already seen, **offering a healthier alternative for those trying to avoid fattening products is essential**, so make sure you always have some light snacks to please this group of customers.

On this site, you will find great oat bars, perfect for dieters, for example, the healthy products from *"Annie's Homegrown Organic"* or *"Back to nature"* line. The products offered by this company are endless, so I highly recommend you look at everything they offer to stock your business with healthy and tasty products.

Also, don't forget to include in your inventory zero drinks, which are a favorite of those who are on a diet but want to enjoy a sweet drink.

Https://www.healthysnacksolutions.com/collections/catalog

For your beverages, make sure, as with food, that you can serve both those who are looking for something sweet to get a treat and those who want something that will allow them faster post-workout recovery, so stock your machines with sugary drinks and sports energy drinks. Although, **BJS is a site that allows you to purchase sports drinks** at reduced prices, you will have to get in touch with them to make arrangements regarding the purchase of large quantities of products to get a net discount on your order.

Https://www.bjs.com/products/sports-and-energy-drinks.jsp

Regarding popular sugary drink brands such as *Pepsi* or *Coca-Cola*, one of the methods of obtaining wholesale prices is to contact the company directly, as in the case of Pepsi, which you will find through their partner-friendly site.

Www.pepsicopartners.com

Each area has a different type of customer base, so before buying products to put in your vending machines, make sure you have conducted good market research.

Once you understand who you are selling to, my advice is to purchase a large quantity of the product you are sure your customers will buy, organizing a stockpile that can accommodate demand.

You will only need a month to understand whether a product is profitable or not: those finished within seven days are highly profitable products, so you will be better off, once you discover them, to stock up on them in large quantities.

However, those that do not sell within one month are products that you can begin to eliminate from your supply. I recommend that you try to run out of stock of that product within two months, and then opt to try to make room for a new product and observe its behavior: remember that **you don't have infinite space in your vending machine**s, so continuing to hold a spot occupied by a product that the public doesn't seem to want will be solely a loss of money for you. If, in its place, you find a product that sells like hotcakes, over the course of a few weeks, you may be able to get back into the expense of sourcing the unwanted product, managing to return to profit.

The products that you fail to sell and that you will find in stock do not have to be considered a significant loss: in addition to being able to consume them yourself, *you could make arrangements with another business, such as a coffee shop, gas station, or any business that deals in selling products*, for this one to buy your leftovers at a lower, more affordable price.

In this way, you will lose some money, but you will make room in the warehouse for a new product that could sell a lot, and you will remove from the machine a product that is not succeeding, getting back some of the money from the initial investment in sourcing it.

If you plan to include non-branded products, consider the importance of familiar flavors to your customers. Let me explain: when we are about to buy a bar from a well-known brand that we have eaten hundreds of times before, the moment we bite into it we will taste a flavor familiar to us, so the chance of being disappointed by the flavor and feeling negative emotions toward the place that sold it to us are zero.

On the other hand, when we try a new candy bar that seems similar to those we have already tasted in the past, it would be a problem if the flavor fails the test.

For this reason, before you put products into your machines that you do not know the taste and opinion of the public, it is advisable to have them tasted by those you know who can give you an honest and reliable judgment and then decide whether to proceed.

There is, however, a point to consider that when we stock our vending machines, deciding to **sell exotic, new-tasting products that the customer has never seen before could be a point of advantage over our competitors**, as customers might opt for our vending machines and all the novelties they offer.

Many people are curious about new snacks and drinks that they could never easily find in retail stores, so when they find a product they have never tried before, they want to give it a chance.

We might change the assortment of specialty products every two weeks or every week so that a visit to your vending machines becomes a regular occurrence for some customers who are curious to find out what's new to try.

When it comes to deciding how to restock your vending machines, one of the techniques that might help you make sure you don't go wrong is to immerse yourself in the action of buying the product:

starting with the salty snack, what drink would be perfect to go with it? And which dessert would satisfy my sweet craving at the end of the meal?

In this way, you can create winning combinations that will be a real upsell for your customers who will come by your machines, for example, to enjoy some chips but who will accompany them with a carbonated drink and finish it off with a dessert.

BJ's, *Costco*, and *Sam's Club* have created membership clubs you can join to get their products in bulk. Alternatively, many e-commerce companies such as Gumball.com, Vistar.com, and Amazon Business present viable alternatives.

The most reliable suppliers in the United States, according to a recent statistical study, are:

1. *Mars Inc*
2. *Wurth Industry North America*
3. *Diebold, Inc.*
4. *Cranemerchandisingsystems*
5. *Glory, Inc.*
6. *R.S. Hughes Co., Inc.*
7. *Apex Supply Chain Technologies*
8. *Cardinaldistributing, Inc*
9. *Fordgum&Machineco, Inc.*
10. *Betson Enterprise*

THE MOST POPULAR DRINKS TO PUT IN YOUR MACHINE

People who buy food will probably decide to spend some money to be able to drink something tasty, cool, and refreshing directly from the place where they purchased their food.

You must have realized how important it is to properly stock your vending machines to ensure maximum customer satisfaction and possible earnings.

Let's now look at the drinks that can never be lacking in your vending machine:

1. **Water is the must-have for every machine.** Water has a small cost for the customer but an easy profit for you: so many people buy water throughout the day to stay hydrated. Remember that there are people out there on diets who force themselves to drink water but are used to sugary drinks. Offer them the option of drinking flavored or carbonated water, so they will choose your machines whenever they are around.

2. Energy drinks are able to give a burst of energy to those who drink them. These are an excellent alternative to coffee. Among energy drinks, some are also healthy and chosen by those who want to avoid sugary drinks. I recommend the brand *Yerbamate, Tenzing, Xite, or Zevia.* Searching in wholesale stores, you will surely find the product you think is best for you.

3. *Iced coffee* is a tasty alternative to plain coffee. Iced coffee is used as a beverage to drink on the way to work, on the way home, or during a walk.

4. Americans love *soda drinks*, which are drunk by 1 in 2 Americans daily. So you will understand how profitable such a product can be, knowing that it is a product that can really go down the drain.

5. *Iced teas*, with wide varieties, both with and without sugar, please many lovers of this flavor. In addition, peach and lemon flavors are a favorite among Americans.

6. *Fruit and vegetable juices* are an excellent choice for vending machines. The most common are sugary, but sugar-free ones are one of the top choices for those who are trying to maintain their figure and enjoy something healthy. The company Liquidline is one example that offers solutions for installing smoothie machines that can provide a freshly squeezed product daily.

7. *Protein shakers* are little machines designed primarily for those who exercise and do not have time to prepare their own protein shaker at home. This is why little machines can

answer this question, such as those from the Bio-Synergy brand, which, if installed near a gym, turn out to be gold mines!

MACHINE PERSONAL HYGIENE PRODUCTS

It happens to everyone to leave home and realize that they have forgotten something important. Those who are traveling, those who need something urgent during their work break, or those who are simply careless will see in your vending machines a real salvation!

Among the non-edible products that you can put in your vending machines are, without a doubt:

1. *Toothbrush and toothpaste*, which you can sell as a combo or separately depending on how you prefer, are a product that will make happy those who may have forgotten them at home and don't know how to brush their teeth.
2. *Deodorants*, for those who have not had time to take a good shower in the morning and have been out of the house for a while, this is a really essential product.
3. *Hand sanitizer* is essential for those traveling by public transportation in times like these.
4. *Sunscreen* is a popular and useful product, especially in tourist areas where it is common to spend the day by the sea.

RESOURCES

Like other sectors, the vending machine business also needs a range of support and resources, such as publications, trade organizations, and developing and researching new technologies.

Indeed, **it is essential to keep up with the times and quickly recognize what is new and changing in an increasingly dynamic market.**

The following websites can give you great help in understanding how best to start your vending machine business:

VENDING MARKET: Website with the latest news and trends concerning the vending machine market, technological innovations, and new equipment.

VENDING TIMES: This online publication gives an overview of what is new and what is trendy in the industry.

VENDSOFT: A software that allows the management of vending machines and offers various supports in managing your business in real time. The *vendsoft* website includes both a blog and a guide with helpful links for developing your business.

National Automatic Merchandising Association was Founded in 1936. This association represents the convenience services industry in the United States. It provides education, research, and support to its more than 1,000 members.

Vending Connection is another great online publication offering news and useful information.

Another important support can be found by comparing yourself with other vending machine owners by joining the various *Facebook* groups dedicated to the topic.

Here are some of the most popular groups:

- *Vending Machine Tips and Discussion* (26.8K members): Very useful private group to ask questions about running a vending machine business. This public group provides a space where both individual vendors and companies can sell machines of different types. This is not a group that deals specifically with vending machines, but it is possible that there are people willing to sell them.
- *Vending Marketplace* (57.3K members): In this public group, owners or renovators of vending machines can sell their devices, their franchises, or their vending machine business.
- *Vending Machine - Buy, Sell, or Get Help* (42.1K members): This private group helps to vending machine owners, and

restorers find the suitable machines and ask questions about their devices.

- *How to Start a Vending Machine Business* (25.2K members): This private group can be helpful for aspiring and new entrepreneurs understand how best to start a successful vending machine business.

FIVE

THE RIGHT SUPPLIER

Your business, to function properly, must be supported by the right supplier. If you need support, you don't have someone on the other side who will supply you with the required product in a reasonable time, and at a fair price. **It will be impossible for you to carry on this business while coming in under cost and making a profit.**

The cost of procurement is not the only factor you need to consider when choosing your future supplier: my advice is to choose one who will undertake to conduct market research for you and source the most suitable product to sell to you, so that the partnership will be long-lasting and profitable for both of you!

Also, remember that you will not be dealing solely with one type of supplier; there are four:

Manufacturers are those who make the product you are selling. This type of solution is the cheapest since you negate entirely the problem of having to pay someone to source large quantities of product for you. Also, if you realize that the audience in your sales area would prefer a specific type of product, you could get in touch with the manufacturer and agree to make it.

1. *Distributors*, those who sell manufacturers' products in bulk, require a minimum order of pieces, which can be very high. From these, you might buy an essential product such as water. In any case, trying to contact the manufacturers is always advisable.
2. *Artisans* are independent workers who sell unique products for specific niches. Their higher-than-average cost can turn out to be a profit if they can find the right product for the right target audience.
3. *Domestic importers* are essential if you want to sell a product only found abroad. You will need to approach a company that can act as a wholesaler and has suitable contacts for importing. Remember, however, that these products are more expensive because of import duties and taxes to be paid.

THE RIGHT SUPPLIER CAN MAKE ALL THE DIFFERENCE

As mentioned above, price is not the only parameter you need to consider when you supply your vending machines. If your supplier is unreliable, you will not be able to carry on business without too many problems.

Supplier reliability includes different parameters. Indeed, finding a supplier who is not committed to meeting deadlines will equate to having unreplenished vending machines and, therefore, not 100% operational.

You cannot afford such a loss of money, so I advise **finding a supplier who has already been working with other businesses for some time and whose reliability you are fairly certain of**. Before proceeding, find out about the supplier's shipping and procurement costs so you understand what price you will have to put the product in the machine at, calculating the cost of the taxes you will have to pay.

Also, consider that during the transportation of the goods, some product may be damaged. In that case, if you have not agreed beforehand with the supplier about what kind of solution you might find to solve the problem, you may find yourself with a damaged product and no refund.

At the point when you buy a product directly from the manufacturer and not from the supplier, *a good move might be to go to their offices and personally check the quality of the production work*, so that the final product you buy may not have any problems that would jeopardize your business.

Another aspect to remember when buying from a supplier is the product's expiration date. This I am about to give you is a tip that could prove to be a win-win for your business: in some cases, products close to the expiration date could be sold by the supplier at a lower price, proving to be a bargain for your business.

The best way to take advantage of this possibility is to find out what kind of product sells the most in your vending machines, **trying to buy it from the supplier at a lower price because of its expiration date.**

If you do your calculations right, you can sell the product at the usual price quickly and before it has expired, paying it at a lower price and margining a higher profit!

Staying on the subject of expired products, **a good supplier who has already worked with other companies can give you good advice on what kind of assortment to buy,** as it is also in his interest that you sell as much product as possible to come back and buy from him, avoiding the purchase of products that are difficult to sell and could easily reach their expiration date.

As we have already mentioned, contacting producers is what will save us the most money since we will not have to pay the supplier, but some companies do not allow direct sales, forcing you to buy the product from wholesalers. In addition, larger companies do not allow the purchase of small quantities of products, so you will have to calculate what are the maximum amounts you need before purchasing concerning the sold- speed of the product and its expiration date.

One way in which you might save money is by purchasing products from foreign suppliers, but not before inquiring about their manufacturing processes and the safety standards adopted, which may not be considered legal in America. In these cases, the main risk lies in the inability to test the product before purchase, so you will have to trust and hope that what you are buying has a quality in line with your expectations.

You must not forget that when you buy from local producers, in addition to being supporting your nation's economy, you have significant advantages: **you can easily verify the supplier and you will not have problems regarding the production processes used**, because the laws in force in America will protect them.

Also, speaking the same language as the supplier is no slight advantage when you are looking to purchase a product, which might be absent if you buy from countries like China. In addition to this, there are quick shipping times, more secure payments, and the possibility of refunds and replacements that are much easier than trading with foreign countries.

To find out if your supplier is trustworthy, you can use social media, as any of them have a history of reviews and opinions from those who have used the service and, in many cases, you will be quickly updated on new products being launched that might interest you to enrich your machine offerings.

Linkedin is a good resource for finding out more about your suppliers.

The easiest way to reach new suppliers is to search online for the product name and then "supplier" or "wholesaler," you'll see that within minutes you'll be able to connect with those who could help you get the business you're creating off the ground.

Tip for being able to find the owner of a domain if you're not sure if the supplier you're relying on is legitimate: You'll find out who owns the website by using whois Lookup to search for the domain you have doubts about.

In addition to just Google, sites like eBay and Amazon contain many suppliers of exciting products that you can include in your inventory. Remember that you don't have to sell food products, so as far as tech gadgets like headphones or chargers are concerned, you can arrange through one of these shops to get a discount.

In addition to these, *Aliexpress* and Alibaba are two great sites to find tech items at bargain prices. *Aliexpress* costs less on average than Amazon, while Alibaba allows you to buy a stock of a product and get big discounts.

Similar to Alibaba, we find Global Sources and Buyer Zone.

Another tip I want to share with you is to **use social and forums to reach out to suppliers and wholesalers**: groups are a great place to expand your network, as they allow you not only to get in touch with suppliers but also to be able to exchange ideas and experiences with others who work in the vending machine world, perhaps recommending a good, reliable supplier or advising you against one, so you won't waste time and money.

Some industry associations, such as the *National Automatic Merchandising Association* or the *Texas Merchandise Vending Association*, are helpful in finding information regarding suppliers and products on trend in America.

To learn about new products and their suppliers, you can start by attending trade shows, where you will meet others who, like you, work in the world of machinery.

THE 10 TIPS THAT WILL SAVE YOU PROBLEMS WITH SUPPLIERS

Any business needs suppliers, but behind suppliers are people who may prove to be unreliable, default and cause you significant economic losses.

That's why I'm now going to suggest a list of points to deal with every time you get in touch with a new supplier that will enable you to avoid surprises in the course of your work.

Yours is a fledgling business, so you may not have immediate cash on hand. Point this out to your supplier, and **seek an arrangement that allows you to defer payments or put them off at least a month after placing the order**. If, on the other hand, you possess the money to pay the supplier in the immediate term, I suggest you seek a bulk purchase discount. Also, negotiate refund terms if the product that arrives does not conform to agreements, perhaps managing to have 60 to 90 days from receipt of the order to get a refund.

1. *Who will pay for the shipping costs of the product?* While you agree on prices, your supplier may not include shipping costs in his final price. Ensure you understand who will bear these costs, so you don't get an unpleasant surprise.

2. *Make sure there is a certificate of liability insurance*: if the product you are buying should be defective or if the machine you purchased should fail, you will need this certificate to request service. You will have to renew this certificate yearly, so ask the supplier to show you the most recent one.

3. *Make sure you can return products that you find do not conform to your business*, as in some cases, it may be necessary. With some suppliers, you may be more convincing by offering credit solutions.

4. *Make sure that the products always arrive on time*, as not being able to restock your machines, as we have already mentioned, results in a loss of money for you. Should there

be a delay in delivery, you can opt to deal with the supplier in two ways: total cancellation of the order so that you can contact another supplier who can meet your request quickly, which will not cost you any loss of money, or you can get a discount on the purchased goods to repay you for the delay. Don't forget to put everything in writing, as a contract is binding, while the given the word is not.

5. *Ask the supplier for advice on pricing the products in your machines*, as he may have more experience in pricing than you do. Consider your costs and decide whether it is worthwhile for you to purchase the product and whether you will have a sufficient profit margin.

6. *Try to understand the reasons why product prices might change*: rising fuel prices, scarcity of raw materials to create the product itself, and increasing gas and electricity costs may affect the production price of the individual product, translating into a higher cost for you. Ask your supplier what factors you might want to keep in check and decide how to act accordingly.

7. *Inquire about any discounts you may receive as a result of buying large quantities of a product*; this way, you can profit much more from the sale.

8. *Inquire about minimum quantities*, as some suppliers do not allow the purchase of small amounts of products. In this case, it is essential to realize how much the minimum can be purchased to understand how to organize one's inventory in relation to the available stock.

9. *Ask the supplier if they have any offers to buy assorted products designed for a business like yours*, so you can save money and fill your vending machines with the right foods.

What I want you to understand with these points is that when we are trying to start a business, and we are not yet experts in the field, there is no such thing as stupid questions. Only questions not asked could lead to serious problems for our income.

Rely on these ten points for no surprises, but don't be afraid to ask the vendor any other questions that cross your mind.

THE METHODS OF NEGOTIATION

It is in your interest and goal to try to lower the prices of the products you purchase to profit as much as possible from their sale.

The relationship you are establishing with your suppliers must last in the long term to benefit both you and the supplier. Reducing your procurement costs is the best way for you to grow and your supplier to sell more products, so leverage this as much as possible!

When you negotiate with your supplier, consider that you are not trying to win a war: you both need to get up from the bargaining table satisfied with the outcome. You can achieve this by agreeing to substantial minimum orders but at lower prices so that the supplier can make a lot of money by selling many products, and you can save money.

We can divide the work you will have to do to negotiate the best deal into five main steps:

1. *Clear your goals so you know how to negotiate to get what is right for you.* We have already seen that the main aspects to consider when buying a stock of products from a supplier are price, delivery time, quality of the product, the possibility of quick maintenance of the machines, the possibility of returning defective products, and by how much you can pay for the stock of products purchased in case you are starting your business and do not have immediate liquidity.

2. *Put yourself in the supplier's shoes-you don't have to be the only one to benefit from bargaining.* Larger suppliers have a much smaller bargaining margin than small companies. Working with many customers, they will always have someone with available cash and willing to pay what they

require. In contrast, a small supplier trying to expand his circle of customers could easily compromise with you.

3. *Don't show up for your appointment with the supplier without a clear plan*: put down a set of points to define with the supplier, clearly stating which aspects are bargainable and which must be as you have envisioned them. During the negotiation, try to emphasize the benefits for the supplier who decides to work with you.

4. *Think of your interlocutor as an expert*: the vendor you will talk to probably already has experience in the field, so you will probably be the one to negotiate his terms, not the other way around. However, there are negotiation techniques common to all vendors that will help you uncover your interlocutor's cards.

One example is rushing you through phrases such as "this product on these terms will no longer be available starting next week, so I suggest you book it today." These phrases create urgency in your psyche, making you think you are about to miss a once-in-a-lifetime opportunity and causing you to fall into the supplier's trap, buying products at a price decided by him, which may not be the cheapest for you. **Another method by which suppliers manage to cheat buyers is by setting the prices of goods very high to offer you a fake discount and make you think you are getting a bargain.** My advice to you to avoid falling into these traps is never to accept the first offer they offer and always try to bargain down.

A good strategy might be to show up for the appointment only after you have done some market research to find out the prices of the goods, so you can understand whether the supplier is giving you a real discount. Don't be greedy! On the other side, you have an entrepreneur who is trying to run a business, just like you, so try to arrive at the most mutually beneficial solution.

Create a contract to ensure that everything agreed upon is adhered to, protecting your business interests and those of the supplier. In addition, the contract should hold you responsible for problems that the product might have once the supplier delivers it, such as in the case of used vending machines that might malfunction after a short time.

It should be clear in the contract how to act if this happens, so make the supplier responsible for these problems so that you always have assistance.

Also, include cancellation clauses in the contract to avoid all kinds of problems should the supplier not behave properly toward you.

Start by inquiring about who the suppliers are in your area so you can save on shipping costs and get in touch with them to get the initial information you need to start your business.

SIX

HOW TO CREATE YOUR BUSINESS STRUCTURE

When you start working on your new business, you will need to be clear on what tax position to place yourself to operate safely and comply with U.S. laws.

Laws can change at the federal and state levels, so you need to find out about the following before you proceed:

1. What kind of *taxes will you have to pay* since some legal entities will consider the earnings from your business as if they were your personal income, while in other cases, they can be considered business income.

2. Depending on what kind of *company you are going to build,* your responsibilities may change: if, for example, you separate your assets from those owned by the company, the state will not be able to seize your personal assets in case it goes bankrupt. If, on the other hand, your business and personal assets are the same thing, the IRS could seize everything in case of trouble. The type of company you are going to set up, as it could have you as the sole manager or have a board of directors or shareholders to whom you will always have to report the progress of your company.

3. *From whom the company's main 'money supply' comes,* which may come from shareholder investors but also from outside sources such as loans from banks, lending institutions, or crowfunding sites. Each person involved in the business project must be registered with an EIN identification number.

These are the five main points for learning how to move in this area, so consider informing yourself to give an answer to any kind of doubts you have about these kinds of aspects before starting your business.

THE TYPES OF COMPANIES

There are essentially four types of companies you can set up to operate legally in the vending machine industry, and we will now look at them together.

1. *Sole proprietorship* requires a natural owner responsible for repaying business debts and collecting business income. In this case, the owner has complete control over all company decision-making processes, so it is much easier to start the business. However, it must be considered that all risks will fall on the owner. Paperwork in this type of business is kept

to a minimum, and costs will be limited to license fees and taxes, which vary depending on the state in which you will operate. When you start your business, inquire about tax deductions intended for sole proprietorships that could save you money. If the business does not go as planned and you want to close, you could do so without any problem since you would not have to confront a partner, but not before making sure you settle all business debts.

2. A *partnership* allows two or more partners to open a business, choosing whether to divide the responsibilities equally through a general partnership or to create a limited partnership, in which one of the partners might do the manual labor. In contrast, the others contribute money to the business.

When you operate as a limited liability company, your assets are separated from the business assets, **preventing the IRS from seizing what is separate from the business should you go bankrupt**.

A partnership is simple to form, requiring little paperwork. Also, since there are more partners, you could earn much more than a sole proprietorship, as you could divide the work and save time. Also, if you do not have sufficient credibility to apply for a bank loan, your partner may have it!

Finally, general partnerships usually do not pay corporate income tax.

1. *A limited liability company* allows the company to take on the identity of an entity in its own right. They can have several partners, and profits and losses are not distributed among them. Instead, the revenues generated by the business go directly into the owners' pockets, without being taxed by the government, which will have to report profits and losses on their tax returns. In this case, hiring a professional to handle the accounts would be useful, although it would involve additional costs. If, on the other

hand, you want to save money, you can carry out the business accounting yourself.

2. *A corporation* is a way to go when the company you are running takes on significant size. This is where shareholders come in, who become owners of a part of the company divided into shares. If the company grows and prospers, the shares increase in value.

Shareholders who own a large part of the company have decision-making power, along with the CEO who is voted in by the board of directors.

There are two solutions here: S-corporations limit the business owner's liability, but is taxed as a partnership (provided there are 100 shareholders or less).

C-corporations are publicly traded and can have unlimited shareholders. Therefore, taxation is double in this case, first on the corporation, then on the individual shareholder.

The advantages of this company are protected from claims against the company, but they have full responsibility for their share invested in the company.

It continues to exist if the company owner pulls out of the business.

It is easier for this type of company to find capital by selling shares, allowing the company to expand quickly.

Choose carefully what kind of business is right for you. Afterwards, talk to your accountant and find a solution that suits yours needs to start operating in the vending machine business with total legality.

PLANNING A BUSINESS PLAN TO SCALE YOUR BUSINESS

Many entrepreneurs do not consider it essential to create a business plan, as the events that happen during a business can be truly unpredictable. No one imagined the arrival of a pandemic and the outbreak of a conflict in 2022, but these are events that really happened and have irrevocably affected economies around the world.

Those who opened a business before the pandemic outbreak

certainly did not anticipate such an event, but they still had to deal with the consequences.

That being said, **a business plan can still help streamline the decisions that need to be made during the operation of your business**, since the moment you have already planned well in advance what kind of growth to implement for your company, it will be easier for you to decide which direction to go in and at what time to do so.

If you decide to draw up a business plan, you will be advantaged in the decision-making process at the time when a big challenge may come along.

In addition, as we have seen in previous chapters, before launching into a business like vending machines you need to understand what kind of product the target audience of the place where you will position your business is looking for: this is also part of planning a good business plan, because it makes you aware of the kind of gap you are trying to fill with the products you want to sell.

We have also talked about the importance of bargaining with the supplier to lower prices when you are buying goods to supply your business: creating your business plan will allow you to organize a strategy suitable for any situation related to product supply, such as in case of lack of capital, delays on the part of the supplier, or misunderstandings. If you do your calculations well, you will always know how to act in each case, avoiding wasting time and money and steadily growing your business.

Also, remember that when looking for someone to finance your business, demonstrating that you are clear about what you are doing and have planned everything will attract investors and make you credible with banks, who may decide to help you with a loan.

HOW DO YOU MAKE A BUSINESS PLAN?

When you sit down to work on your business plan, you will find yourself thinking about several expenses, ideas, and solutions that could affect the success of your business. As you do this, it is likely that, as you have in front of you all the costs that your business will incur, you will realize that you need to save on some expenses, perhaps opting for a used or conditioned machine instead of a new one as you were sure you could.

There are five main points to discuss in your business plan, and now let's look at them together.

The Executive Summary is written last but is at the beginning of the document; it is used to get a quick idea of what you will talk about in your business plan. The topics you will talk about should be your company's vision, what kind of business model it will have, the products you choose to sell, who you have decided to sell to, and the strategies you will adopt to sell more.

1. *A business overview* that lets those reading your business plan know who they are dealing with in an instant. This overview makes you highly recognizable, so now is the time to include your logo and the colors you will adopt for your business. Try to detach yourself from the image of your competitors; you need to stand out as unique to those who are deciding whether you are worth the risk by investing in you.

2. A *section devoted to the product or service you are offering the customer.* Here you should present the research that led you to realize that a product might interest customers. For example, in the case of niche vending machine products, you need to specify how they might be associated with other products you sell, such as a niche beverage being sold alongside a typical snack. Here you must also indicate your research on production processes, which you will have understood through your contacts with suppliers, and ensure that there are no legal or health violations in making the product.

3. The biggest section of your business plan is the *marketing section*, in which you will have to analyze your competitors, show your market research, your strategies for selling more than your opponents, explain what kind of gap your

business aims to fill, show that there are customers who are asking for a product that is not yet on the market and that you will sell.

4. Once you have identified your competitors, list their *strengths and weaknesses* and specify what you intend to overcome, whether in their strengths or in their weaknesses. Also part of the marketing section is the advertising strategy you will adopt to sponsor your machines: flyers posted near workplaces and schools that could use your product, ads on social media, or any other tactics you intend to adopt should be specified here.

5. *Specify who will be part of your business team.* For example, if you are running a single vending machine business, you may not need assistance right away. Still, if you expand your business, you will be forced to hire people to collect the money, restock the machines, clean the environment, and ensure the machines are operating at 100 percent of their capacity, taking care of repairs if necessary. As for accounting and product counting, there is special software to help you manage this, saving you time and preventing mistakes.

6. The last section relates to the *company's finances*, an element of interest to those who are thinking of investing in your business: show that you can make a profit in a few years, that you have done your research well, and that you know your business will be able to make good profits in a short time. When you do this, remember that it is always better to underestimate earnings than to overestimate them not to disappoint investors.

This type of activity can be very complex, as any business strategy takes time and mental energy to work out.

If you want to make this process less complex, you could consult an accountant to help you define some points of your business plan, particularly from the point of view of economics and permits to be obtained to start the business.

A more significant initial expense invested in an accountant can turn out to be a significant savings of money and time, in the long run, thanks to all the legal and economic problems you will not have to face.

SEVEN

THE IMPORTANCE OF BRANDING

THE NAME: YOUR BRAND'S CALLING CARD

I am sure you have seen dozens of vending machine businesses in your life, not noticing the differences between them, as each one is nothing more than a vending machine.

So how do we differentiate ourselves from the other businesses doing the same thing we are trying to do?

The name is one of the most differentiating elements we can use to create space between us and others.

If you were to read the name *"Kratom Crazy Sprinkles Cupcake Vending Machine on a vending machine,"* what would you think you were about to buy? Obviously, really good cupcakes are intended for a food-loving public that we know frequents the area of our business and who, at non-working hours, would like to enjoy an excellent home-made cupcake!

"Plan B Contraceptive Vending Machines" is a name that speaks for itself: are you looking for a morning-after pill and want to buy it discreetly? Here's your solution! This machine in Southampton is located near Shippensburg University, where there is a high concentration of students, target age customers for this type of product.

We also talked about a machine that can create a copy of your house key in a minute, storing your fingerprint! Oneminutekey is a perfect name to remember what kind of service it offers and how quickly it does it.

In these cases, the name gives an identity to the vending machine, which would be just a machine dispensing product. **With a name of its own it becomes something more, and the customer will remember its existence the moment they need a cupcake or morning-after pill.** This phenomenon is called Brand Recall, and it involves getting into the target customer's mind, becoming the first choice they will think of when they need a product you sell.

If your name is fun, creates interaction and is Instagrammable, it might happen that one of your customers will tag you on social media, sharing your business with others and giving you free publicity.

As a final tip, come up with a name that is short and encapsulates the goal of your business so that it is easy for the customer to remember.

<u>When deciding on a business name, remember to check the domain name on the Internet so you don't risk paying penalties to someone who has already purchased it and owns the rights to it.</u>

The United States Patent and Trademark Office site will allow you to confidently check this aspect of your business. Once you find out that your future name is available, purchase the domain from Google Domains, Godaddy, or any other site that can sell it to you.

At this point, you can create a social media account with your name that will represent your company.

Try to keep your name short and easy to pronounce, and ask friends and family for their honest opinion. If people read your name easily, it will be easy for them to pronounce and remember it. That way, when they feel like eating something good from your machine, they will remember your name and easily find your company online.

Watch out for trends! If there is a trend right now on which you want to base your business name, consider that over time it may fade away, and your customers may no longer connect with your brand. Instead, choose a name that can grow with the customer and be liked for years to come.

Use SEO research to find a list of keywords associated with the food and beverage industry and try to include them in the business name. This will give you greater visibility on search engines. Also, if you have a blog or website include as many keywords as possible so your future customers will easily find you.

If you are imaginative, create a new word not included in the dictionary that will set you apart from others, make you original, and wring a laugh out of the customer. Then, the more they talk about you, the more they will think of you!

One of the ways that a vending machine owner has to make his machines highly visible to the public is to use colors to make the machine immediately recognizable. One example is the pink vending machines that stand out in American airports by Benefit Cosmetics.

This color choice makes the product stand out, in contrast to the flattening colors of other businesses in the airport.

So do M&M and CocaCola, thanks to their yellow and red dispensers, designed to attract the public's attention.

Also, don't forget that you can use your dispenser to interact with the customer through messages placed on it that ask for a review, invite them to take advantage of a special offer, ask them to sign up for a newsletter.

EIGHT
MARKETING FOR YOUR BUSINESS

How could you increase the sales of your business while maximizing its turnover?

To answer this question, we rely on the valuable advice provided by ten industry experts to put into practice every day to ensure the success of your business!

Give the consumer a compelling reason to choose to consume from you.

According to IdealSpot founder and CMO Bryan Eisenberg, those who want to set up the best marketing for a business must first put themselves in a position to give shoppers good reasons to choose their store.

A good idea to make your business visible to possible customers is to **organize events near your business**, such as a small concert or an art exhibition. This might result initially in an expense, but people who come to the event will find out about the existence of your vending machines, considering them for a possible future need for food or drink.

Creating limited offers on certain items on your vending machines can also result in the acquisition of new customers and the purchase of other non-discounted products.

It is not enough to limit yourself to these activities. However, you need to establish a more comprehensive store marketing strategy that will enable you to acquire and retain customers without depending solely on discounts or other promotional activities.

As we have already seen, to do this, you need to:

- understand **who the potential customers are** and what their needs are,
- study the competition and **what they offer**,
- carefully choose the **products and services to sell**,
- leverage strengths and **prevent or correct any weaknesses**,
- build **loyalty among acquired customers.**

To this end, conducting a market analysis certainly comes in handy.

Focus on how to sell products

According to Retail Prophet founder and author of The Retail Revival Doug Stephens, to increase sales, you must first focus on how to market the products of the business being managed. Therefore, we start with a twofold but unequivocal assumption:

- No one really needs what they buy because, in the last 25 years, we have moved from an economy based on scarcity of goods and services to one focused on abundance. This may not be the case with your vending machines because food falls into the indispensable product categories, but *you could also sell nonessential items such as action figures, key chains, sex toys or any other kind of product;*
- Everything is also purchasable through competition. Combining these two points of view, it becomes clear that

the only way to thrive within your market is to differentiate the shopping experience offered to the customer by *offering that extra something that can drive them to your business.*

- Attend to even the smallest details. For brand-building expert, speaker, and author of What Great Brands Do Denise Lee Yohn, those who want to understand how to increase sales in a store must necessarily do everything possible to attend to even the smallest details of the store. **Every single activity must be handled with manic attention**, making the customer perceive the unquestionable excellence conveyed by the brand.

- *Keep researching.* As Retail Minded founder and publisher Nicole Leinbach teaches, a business's success largely depends on the owner's always willing to research what they need to improve their entrepreneurial vision and managed business. Such research can address any area-from sales and inventory to competition, old and new customers, employees to hire or marketing techniques to leverage. Staying current and aiming higher day by day through knowledge is essential to maximizing the chances of success.

- Push customers to take a specific action. Since we're talking about marketing for a winning store, we can't forget the valuable advice provided by The Lion'esque Group founder and author of The Pop-Up Paradigm Melissa Gonzales, who urges merchants to push customers toward taking a specific action at a specific time frame. When shoppers are short on time (scarcity principle), they are pressured by the urgency factor, so they are more enticed to spend. This is because (unconsciously) **they are stimulated to think that that juncture may offer an opportunity that cannot be found at other times.** In other words, you need to give good motivation to act right away. For example, your motivation might be a timed discount on a highly sought-after product by customers.

- Increase local awareness. In the opinion of Sr. editor of Retail Customer Experience James Bickers, to increase sales of a business, it is necessary to become known locally. In fact, the *successful retailer is the one who is, among other things, familiar with the surrounding community*: he is familiar with the people in it, knows what the individual wants, and is aware of the business habits of competitors.
- Don't hide behind the fact that you run a small store. For Global Purchasing Companies, founder Mercedes Gonzales, a business owner who aspires to growth, must never and for no reason in the world hide behind the fact that he runs a small store. To meet with success, this same owner must **give customers a reason to buy and buy back into his business and never tire of doing so.** Succeeding in this is, for example, possible when the offer made available to spenders is useful, unique and limited.
- Having an offline and online presence. As RetailGeek founder and GVP Commerce Strategy at Razorfish Jason Goldberg explains, a store's success depends on both the services-products offered to the public and the image of the business itself projected online. This is primarily because more than half of today's shoppers use digital pre-shop tools, but *the vast majority of those shoppers still prefer to make their purchases in the actual store.*

NINE

THE TECHNICALITIES OF YOUR BUSINESS

LAWS YOU NEED TO KNOW TO START YOUR BUSINESS

Obtaining the necessary permits to start a vending machine business takes time: once you have decided what kind of business you want to open, you will need to apply for your Employer Identification Number (EIN), which, unlike your Social Security number, will be related to your business. This number will be helpful for banks to check that you are in good standing with the IRS, although, in general, it is not mandatory to have an EIN if yours is a sole proprietorship.

To get your EIN, you will need to incorporate your business, visit the EIN Assistant website, follow the process and make the application.

You will need an EIN the moment you hire an employee, become a corporation or partnership, or your business is subject to excise taxes. The last case happens when you sell tobacco, alcohol, or firearms).

Banks expect you to have an EIN when you generate your profits and apply for a credit card linked to your business. Also, without an EIN, you will not be able to apply for a business loan.

As mentioned above, without an EIN, you will not be able to hire employees, as you will not be able to register payrolls with the Internal Revenue Service.

Should you choose to create a limited liability company, the EIN will allow you to separate from your business, so you will avoid making your business debts personal debts.

Among the payments you will owe are sales and use tax payments.

The former is the tax paid to the state when you sell specific goods, while the use tax, similar to sales tax, is levied on services and goods that the business purchases and uses and is exempt from payment once the sale has occurred.

To better understand what kind of taxation is levied and on what products, let's look at the current laws in New York State. According to Tax Bulletin ST-280, food and beverage sales occurring in vending machines are usually **taxed in the same way as they would be if sold in regular grocery stores.**

Sales of food and beverages from vending machines are generally taxed in the same way as sales of the same items in grocery stores. This means that items that are exempt from sales tax when sold in a grocery store are also exempt when sold from a vending machine.

However, there are some exceptions to be aware of. For example, hot drinks sold from a vending machine are exempt from taxation.

Products sold for $1.50 or less are also exempt from taxation if vending machines accept only cash and coins. On the other hand, if the vending machine accepts all forms of payment, the value may be $2 or less.

Taxable foods include sandwiches, foods arranged on a plate or prepared and ready to eat, and foods heated or kept hot in the vending machine (e.g., soups, but this does not apply to broth or any other hot beverage).

Unheated foods (other than sandwiches and other prepared foods), such as whole fruit, cookies, doughnuts, pastries, cereal bars, granola bars, and diet bars, are exempt from sales tax when sold from a vending machine, regardless of their price.

Foods such as pretzels, popcorn, chips, plain or salted nuts, crackers, ice cream, fruit bars, fruit snacks, single-serving cereal packets, and canned foods fall into this category.

Other products include candies and sweets, chocolate bars, chewing gum, honey-roasted nuts and peanuts, popcorn, and pretzels.

Regarding beverages, milk, chocolate milk, diet shakes, vegetable juices, and fruit drinks containing at least 70 percent natural juice fall into this category, too, along with iced tea and coffee, soda, lemonade, sports drinks, and bottled water.

Unless otherwise noted, all products or equipment used to operate the vending machine business are taxable, but it is best to **check with your state's Internal Revenue Service** to ensure this is the case.

General business supplies such as laptops, cell phones, office equipment, cleaning supplies, and computer software fall into this category, along with water, electricity, internet, postage, gas, etc.

Taxable expenses include insurance on the business, security services, vending machine repair or maintenance costs, purchase of new or used vending machines, and anything else that falls under this type of expense.

You are not required to pay sales tax to suppliers for goods for resale because you will pay sales tax when you file your tax return during tax season. However, you must provide the supplier with a completed ST3 exemption certificate and specify that you intend to resell the goods. If you end up paying sales tax on the resale, you can deduct the sales tax paid on your tax return.

This is just an example of the type of taxation in force. To find out the situation in your country, consult the tax bills Food and food products sold by grocery stores and similar establishments (TB-ST-283),

Sandwiches (TB-ST-835), and Beverages sold by grocery stores, beverage centers and similar establishments (TB-ST-65).

These items are taxable if sold from a vending machine at a price above $1.50 or $2, depending on as mentioned above. Remember, you can't include bottle deposits in the calculation of the taxable base.

If you sell taxable food or beverages, you must collect sales tax. You must also register for sales tax and file a tax return to remit the tax collected.

THE BANK ACCOUNT THAT'S RIGHT FOR YOU

If you decide to set up a limited liability company, opening a business bank account can be a good solution for your needs, so you can separate your personal finances from your business finances and easily file your tax return since you will have all business expenses and earnings separate from your personal ones.

A Net 30 account is convenient for those in your position since it is a business line of credit that allows you to purchase assets immediately and pay off the entire balance within 30 days.

Not only do banks disburse Net 30 accounts, but banks offer the convenience of reporting all payments to business credit unions, raising your company's credit profile. This is a double-edged sword, because the moment you do not pay your debts, you will have a report on your company's credit profile.

An alternative is a business credit card, which you can apply for with the help of your banking provider. If used properly, it can help you build your company's credit profile, increasing your chances of financing.

Let's now look at the best banking institutions to consult if you have a small business:

1. *Navy Federal Credit Union* allows small businesses to choose from three different checking accounts, with a 0.5 percent interest rate, and free of charge for the first 30 non-electronic transactions (thereafter, there is a fee of $0.25 per

transaction). A personal account is required to open this account, and membership in someone who is working or retired from the armed forces is needed.

2. The recommended online bank is *Bluevine*. It has no physical branches, but it has excellent online support. It allows you to do all your transactions online and do a few cash transactions per month, you will have an online checking account with no monthly fees and no funds constraints, and you can make a transfer at any time. If your balance exceeds $1,000, you will get 1% interest.

3. *Chase Bank* is great if you will have to run a cash machine, collect the money from your machine every week and deposit it into your bank account. This is where having a physical bank to rely on for cash deposits will be essential, with its 4,700 branches across the United States, more than 16,000 ATMs to choose from, and relatively low fees. However, if you link multiple accounts, you will have higher interest rates.

4. If you want a loan, turn to *SBA Wells Fargo* because of benefits such as small business lending, in which this bank specializes. In addition, you will be able to take out different types of accounts and access payroll services.

5. *US Bank* is a no-fee business checking account that provides net monthly savings and is helpful in the first few months of operation when income is still low. It offers several services, including fraud protection.

Before choosing your future bank, find out which solution is right for you, especially if you are unsure of the immediacy of earnings and your ability to cover the monthly banking costs right away.

LICENSES AND PERMITS YOU CAN'T DO WITHOUT

The costs of running a business like this can change depending on the state or county. Therefore, before you start, you need to check with your local authorities to make sure you have the necessary licenses and permits.

Licensing and permit costs also vary depending on what you are trying to sell with your vending machines. For example, **there are states where you will need to have two separate licenses to sell food and drink.**

Licenses and permits are divided into *Federal*, *State*, and *Municipal* permits. When you start a business, you may not need Federal permits because Municipal permits will be all you need.

Let's see in what kinds of situations you will need federal permits:

- If you will be selling certain foods and beverages, your business must comply with federal, state, and local regulations.
- The FDA district office and local authorities will answer any questions about what kind of beverages and foods you can sell in the state where you work.
- The Americans with Disability Act (ADA) requires the installation of every dispenser respecting mobility disabilities, allowing everyone to access the service easily.
- At the state level, permits and licenses change depending on your state. The location of the vending machine causes certain rules to apply-for example, **if you place a vending machine in a school, you cannot sell alcohol, tobacco, or drugs** (like vending machines selling marijuana, legal in different States). In Florida, every vending machine must have a license, without which you risk closure or a fine. - If you sell products that are not taxable or from 1 priced below 15 cents in California, you will not have to apply for permits to open your business.
- In Arizona, regulations regarding vending machines have changed due to a policy to combat childhood obesity, prohibiting vending machines from selling foods of minimal nutritional value. **Only water and juice can be dispensed in schools and never sold during mealtimes.**

- In Massachusetts, you must have a license issued by the commissary, which will assign you a label to display on the vending machine.

Laws regulating vending machines are also regulated by the city itself, as some cities require a vendor's license, resale permit, or a local food service license to sell products in vending machines.

If you want to be sure of the current laws in your city, contact the city office and ask for assistance regarding your project.

THE IMPORTANCE OF CONTRACTS

When you make arrangements with another contractor in order to supply your business, nothing is as essential as having a solid contract to assure you that everything should go smoothly. <u>If you have written the agreements, the moment the supplier fails to behave properly, you will be protected by the law.</u>

Remember that there are also contractors out there who seek easy profits at their fellow man's expense, so a contract can save you from many problems related to fraudulent contractors.

Among the most common contacts are the rental one, through which you can borrow a machine from another entrepreneur or the manufacturing company for an agreed-upon period of time that may renew; the service one, to be signed by suppliers, machine operators, and insurance companies, serves to make clear the type of business relationship you are creating.

You can use the certificate of occupancy to confirm that you have complied with all building codes and regulations.

Another essential contract that you need to draw up is the one with the owner of the property you will be renting to place your vending machines: the costs of utilities and rent should be very clear, and they should not vary depending on events that could increase their costs (as has been happening recently due to conflicts).

The contracts you enter into with the vending machine manufacturers are also useful to protect you in the event of a

vending machine failure. This is the way you can ensure that you will always have someone capable of replacing a defective part, and you can determine who should be charged for the cost of the damage from the outset.

You'll find free contract templates online, but talk to your lawyer to ensure you're doing it right by submitting the contract to him or her and making any necessary changes.

In the next chapter, we'll look at how to create an insurance contract that allows you to cover any damage to the structure and let you sleep soundly.

TEN

BUSINESS AUTOMATIZATION

HOW TO AUTOMATE YOUR BUSINESS

Let's now consider an essential element of your business that could save you a lot of time: after the initial phase, the foundations of your business are established, and you will face a more or less significant number of decisions to make and which you will have to manage.

It can be complicated to be able to conduct such processes when you have to manage several stores, so automation is needed.

Automation is a phase you can implement in any type of

company in all its sectors and activities. It is not so much about expanding as it is about improving the efficiency of what already exists.

All of this is necessary because every company, as the market evolves, must adapt to demand, new service supplies, and new demands, making it essential to have a certain speed and efficiency in adapting to the changing world, which can only be achieved through automation.

<u>The goal is company growth, but this cannot happen immediately and without a solid growth plan behind it.</u>

It is crucial to identify which steps are slowing down the production process early, because they are perhaps now obsolete or inadequate to meet demand and to know how to intervene consciously.

This is where automation, in its various forms, can prove crucial to improving efficiency and contributing to your company's growth.

These are some suggestions that will enable you to automate and grow your business more effectively:

1. *Find out which areas or processes can be made simpler.* Inventory, managing communication with suppliers, creating budgets, and monthly reports, or even organizing marketing can be a problem of lack of organization or slowness, which takes away a lot of valuable time. This is why it is necessary to immediately identify the weak link in the chain and take the proper measures. If it takes time to communicate what supplies you are out of, organize an Excel file that encapsulates the appropriate spreadsheet windows to manage your inventory so that you promptly know how much merchandise you need. An organized Excel spreadsheet will be indispensable for carrying on accounts and writing your monthly report.

2. *Formulate standard operating procedure.* It is good to draw up the steps for carrying out the procedures that will be essential to your business. In this case, it would be best to be as precise as possible in order to identify the element that

slows down the entire process and figure out which steps will be possible to automate.

3. *Identify repetitive activities.* Once the various steps in each process are placed under scrutiny, check which ones can be eliminated as unnecessary or too cumbersome. In fact, the goal is to make the entire process as least cumbersome as possible by removing anything that can be considered an obstacle.

4. *Understanding and analysis of procedures.* After reviewing the different mechanisms once again, start thinking about where you can replace the human element with software or an otherwise automated process without the entire supply chain being compromised.

5. *Research and use the software that best suits your business.* First, not all software is very expensive; you can even find some that cost a few dollars a month (of course, this depends on the functionality and the task software is meant to perform). Generally, a free trial period is guaranteed for each software so that you can figure out whether what you intend to purchase fits with your goals.

EASILY AUTOMATED BUSINESS TASKS

While there are some tasks where human labor is a must, there are not a few steps within a vending machine business that can be handled automatically by software:

- *Email and social media*: several apps and tools are available on the market that allow you to manage your online presence automatically. These tools will take care of advertising, tracking visitors, capturing new audiences, and building trust with regular customers. The algorithms in these applications will generally make sure that your brand and business reach as many people as possible, allowing you to create a specific image and reputation. Mailchimp is an example of a valuable platform to manage to send emails to your target audience, which will save you a lot of time.

- *For billing and accounting,* there's software that's right for you, taking complete care of your accounting; it will automatically track receipts, invoices, and calculate taxes, monthly budgets, income, and expenses. Some more advanced software can even generate reports and forecasts. *Netsuite* and *Freshbooks* are two excellent examples of software suitable for managing your accounts.

- *You could need to transfer files,* and through digital tools, it is possible to go paperless for any kind of documentation regarding a business. Here again, there are several options available-Google, WeTransfer, Dropbox are just a few among several choices that are available on the Web. With limited access, you can also store gigabytes of files and data in the Cloud.

- The ability to use a single online platform to *communicate and work with employees,* suppliers, and any type of professional figure that ensures the functioning of a company is crucial. I advise using Telegram to manage your team and communicate with your suppliers. This is because telegram stores old files, allowing you to access them at any time, and could come in handy when you need to find an old contract, logo, or any other file sent in a telegram chat.

- There is different software that could prove indispensable to the management of your business. For example, *Vend-track,* an application on which you can have a 14-day free trial of some of its functions, allows you to control and manage different aspects of your business, especially if you have multiple vending machines scattered in multiple locations. *Vending Machine Sistem (VMS)* is especially recommended for the more experienced and allows you to check the progress and performance of vending machines in real time, monitoring and alerting you when you need to replenish products. Although not the simplest of programs,

Cantaloupe allows for great optimization in managing your distributors, as it allows you to manage inventory and logistics, as well as a charge by both paper and mobile devices.

- *Quickbooks* could be convenient to use. It has an app that allows it to be used on both PCs and other devices, with a Cloud that ensures secure data storage, as well as keeping track of income and expenses and creating customizable invoices. Unfortunately, not a few companies in the industry use this platform. Although we are talking about a business that in itself requires a high level of automation, once the earnings start coming in and consequently there is growth in the business, you will need to start considering hiring people to do certain jobs, such as the *quality check* of your products. One area where staffing is necessarily required is assessing the quality of goods, identifying defective products, and ensuring prescribed levels of safety and hygiene. In this case, it will be good to carefully select one's employees to make the work as efficient as possible and minimize all potential problems.
- *Customer support* is essential for your business. You, or someone trained by you, must be available to intervene as promptly as possible in case of theft or malfunctioning the vending machines with possible reimbursements.
- *All* machines, even the most advanced, can experience breakdowns that require *maintenance*. You may consider initially assigning this task to an outside operator and perhaps hiring a repair worker in-house.

Get organized to manage these aspects of your business, one item at a time. I recommend that you start operating only when you know how to handle these kinds of problems so that you never have to offer bad service to your customers.

ELEVEN

CORPORATE INSURANCE OVERVIEW

When starting any kind of business, one must always consider what is called business risk.

Such risk not only looms over equipment and machinery but also over the lives and health of employees, those who enable the business to go forward through their efforts, devoting part of their time, and expending energy and resources.

In order to cope with such risks and protect themselves from the damage that could result, many companies choose to take cover with insurance coverage; in particular, many startup owners find it very useful to protect themselves from events or **impediments that could**

cause more or less serious economic damage by impeding the growth of their business.

The functionality and usefulness of insurance coverage is demonstrated by the fact that, even though it is not mandatory, many commercial enterprises independently decide to take out some type of insurance.

This expense is made in order to have a guarantee of protection against damaging or adverse events.

For example, damage done by vandals to your vending machines or an unexpected lawsuit are events that could do more significant damage to your business if there were not some form of insurance coverage.

In fact, **the lack of the latter would mean shelling out larger sums of money that could significantly affect your business.**

It is essential to know that there is no single form of insurance protection because the offered solutions are varied and diverse.

Moreover, the reasons why it is advisable to take out an insurance contract are not exclusively related to vandalism or lawsuits, and now we will look at what are the cases that might lead you to need insurance:

1. *Insurance in case of natural disaster or property damage. You can install v*ending machines either inside or outside a building. However, suppose the roof of the building in which your vending machine is located sustains damage due to the weather. In that case, you may have to pay for the damage to allow your business to continue to be functional and welcoming. Insurance can help you with problems like this, so consider protecting yourself from natural disasters.

2. *Insurance for managing economic crises or uncertainties about the future.* The covid-19 pandemic has been a perfect example of how many companies, due to the various lockdowns, have seen their revenues drop dramatically, if not forced out of business. Only companies with insurance could seek compensation that allowed them to survive in

some way. In a world that is increasingly dynamic and subject to change, with unforeseen events always just around the corner and an increasingly interconnected world market, various forms of insurance allow companies to be able to succeed in curbing problems related to the sudden cessation of business or loss of revenue for whatever reason.

3. *Possibility of saving money in the long run.* While an insurance policy means adding an additional monthly expense to the set of costs you face, it also means protecting yourself from far more burdensome expenses to shell out in the event of an adverse event of whatever nature it may be. It is always preferable to pay a fixed monthly fee to protect yourself rather than find yourself borrowing or shelling out large amounts of money to pay for damages, injuries, accidents, and whatnot.

4. *Request for insurance coverage from lending institutions.* When applying for a loan to expand your business, the financial institution you have applied to will likely ask you to submit documents of an insurance policy. This way, the bank ensures that the money you are applying for will actually be invested in the project. An insurance policy then acts as a kind of guarantee of what your venture is and what your goals are.

5. *Peace of mind resulting from insurance coverage.* When a large company suffers an economic setback, it generally already has all the tools it needs to deal with it. Unfortunately, the same cannot be said for small businesses, which, indeed, short of economic rescue, will be able to recover much more slowly, and without the certainty of succeeding. This is precisely why insurance coverage offers small business owners the opportunity to have a support network in case of need or difficulty.

INSURANCE FOR VENDING MACHINES

There are some special risks associated with the vending machine business, including:

- *Theft and vandalism*, particularly for those machines placed in public areas and therefore accessible to anyone;
- *Malfunctioning of machines*, which require maintenance;
- Credit card fraud;
- *Harm to patrons*, which can be caused by the quality of the products sold, as in the case of food poisoning following the consumption of a product purchased from one of your vending machines.

That is why there are different forms of insurance for the vending machine business that can implement protection even though it is not always possible to get full protection due to the unaffordable cost of insurance policies.

But don't worry. There are three types of insurance policies that are able to provide you with maximum coverage:

- **Commercial general liability insurance** can be considered the most comprehensive type of insurance. It manages to cover bodily injury, property damage, accident payments, losses resulting from false claims in advertisements, and expenses associated with lawsuits and legal judgments.
- **Property insurance** provides protection for the company's assets, such as inventory, storage, or equipment, from loss or damage. The amount of the insurance policy depends on the size and where the property is located, the value of the inventory, and the value of the vending machines. In addition, some insurance contracts offer BOP (Business Owner's policy), combining property and commercial general liability insurance into a single package.

- **Commercial auto insurance** is helpful if you use a vehicle to transport inventory, restock vending machines, and perform other business-related activities. You can insure the vehicle against traffic accidents, theft of the car, or medical expenses for injuries sustained by the driver during transport. Even if you use a personal vehicle, it is always advisable to take out an insurance policy related to the transportation of auto goods, as many personal car insurances do not cover accidents or business-related expenses.

If you want to safeguard yourself further, for added security, there are other insurance policies available that can be considered:

- **Workers' compensation policy** covers your company's workers against work-related injuries. In addition, this policy covers medical expenses or compensation regarding days of absence due to illness or injury.
- **Crime insurance** protects against criminal acts such as theft or vandalism. This type of protection is important since these are the most real and looming threats to your business.
- **Business interruption insurance**, which is useful in the event of business closure not due to your will. This type of insurance will compensate you for lost economic income due to the closure of the business itself.
- **Product liability insurance** kicks in if one of the products you sell causes physical harm to customers.

This type of insurance will cover both legal and medical expenses for injured clients.

COSTS AND CONSIDERATIONS REGARDING INSURANCE COVERAGE

An important element influencing the choice of which insurance to take out is the cost.

Insurance agencies set rates based on a number of variables: size of the business, the area where vending machines are located, the value of equipment, and the degree of risk you are exposed to.

To establish a budget regarding insurance, you can consider the parameters below: a commercial car insurance policy may base its premium on the car's model and the driver's license type. The premium varies between $750 and $1,250 per month.

As for workers' compensation insurance, the premium varies, considering the number of employees and the type of benefit to be offered to them. It varies in percentage ranging from 3 to 5 percentage points of an employee's salary.

As for the premium for general liability insurance, it is based on the company's turnover. If you bill, for example, $1,000 a year, this can result in insurance coverage ranging from $400 to $500 a month.

It is important not to stop at the first insurance proposal, rather make a comparison of the different offers and quotes that are presented to you.

The goal is to take out insurance that aims to cover you as much as possible rather than to save you money.

Also, if you are struggling with the different clauses or cannot understand them, the advice is to enlist the support of a good lawyer to guide you through the various quibbles and fuzzy areas of the contract.

To save some money and not spend unwise, here are my latest tips:

- Not ensure all the products you sell within your distributor, but only those that could actually cause harm to a customer;
- Insuring a vending machine bought used and with many years behind it can prove to be a counterproductive move because insurance prices for older vending machines often tend to be higher. If, on the other hand, you took the vending machine with a leasing contract, inquire about the

type of insurance the company that sold you the machine offers.

- If the place where you have placed your vending machines is in a central or constantly frequented area, thus highly exposed to the eyes of passersby, you might not even take out coverage for theft and vandalism;
- Choose a policy that is inexpensive and does not have comprehensive coverage.

TWELVE

GETTING STARTED WITH A LOAN

CALCULATE THE INITIAL EXPENSES FOR STARTING THE BUSINESS

Before making any kind of purchase, signing any sort of contract, before anything, it is good to start by considering your budget, how to spend it, and how to go about it.

For example, in buying a vending machine, it is good to do some preliminary personal research, and comb through marketplaces or dedicated groups on social networking sites such as Facebook. Then, after you figure out the purchase costs, you can understand what solutions might be right for you and what is the most convenient.

Here is a list of what might be the initial expenses, those necessary to be able to start your vending machine business, keeping in mind that other expenses might always be there. That is why it is always good to do some initial research to figure out how much money you will need.

- *Refurbished snack and beverage vending machine: $2000-3000*
- *Stockpile area: $100 per month*
- *Transportation and related costs: $50-100 per month*
- *Routine maintenance: $50-250 per year*
- *Taxes: 10-37% of declared gross income*
- *Commissions for card purchases: 5-6% per sale*
- *General liability insurance: $300-1000 per year*
- *Brand: $500*

MASTER PLAN FOR COST CONTROL

Cost control refers to the need to reduce any costs considered unnecessary or superficial as much as possible. In practice, it helps to deal with only those expenses necessary to run one's business.

Different from cost control is cost management: this relates to a budget for costs by having monthly recurring expenses as a reference.

Cost control is practical when, for example, one notices that in a month, the expenditure has been higher than what was budgeted, thus allowing one to take action to identify and find ways to eliminate excess expenses.

In your cost control system, you will slowly learn how to streamline your monthly budget more and more. This does not mean eliminating expenses or making choices that save you money, but understanding how to create a realistic budget while also understanding how to move around by finding the best deals, taking advantage of discounts and reward programs, and constantly monitoring expenses.

Here is a list of practical ways to better control business costs:

1. *Understanding the numbers.* The financial forecasts that you

have put within the business plan are those that you will need to keep as a reference each time you calculate expenses and earnings at the end of the month. To avoid negative repercussions, expenses must be less than or at most equal to those that have been budgeted. Sometimes an increase in expenses is not due to unnecessary costs as much as an increase in the price of products, or transportation. Becoming familiar with numbers is important to keep budgets in order.

2. *Taking time to prepare the budget.* The monthly budget is a true cost management plan for a given period, covering both expenses and earnings. These are not simply estimated. When making a plan for cost control, items such as inflation, taxes, and miscellaneous expenses are to be considered. Asking for quotes from suppliers and considering them is also key to keeping costs down, as is knowing the offers on various products and goods.

3. *Monitor inventory.* Having run out of stock is not suitable for your business. Still, the same will be true if you have excess: in the first case, you risk not being able to refill vending machines on time or adequately, resulting in lost earnings; in the second case, on the other hand, the unsold product actually turns into a useless expense. In this case, using suitable software is ideal for keeping an eye on the number of stocks at all times and understanding when it is time to replenish and when to stock up from the supplier.

4. *Minimize repairs (when possible).* Before buying a vending machine, especially a used one, it is a good idea to check its condition, that it is fully functional in all its parts, and that it meets all quality criteria. Constantly calling a technician or even being forced to keep the vending machine closed for repairs will undoubtedly affect costs and generate losses.

5. *Employ strategies to manage time efficiently.* The better you are able to manage your time, the greater your productivity and revenues will be while reducing expenses. In order to

better efficiently manage your time, the path of automation is the most recommended: purchasing software that takes care of the administrative, marketing or other activities that can be done automatically is a great example of efficient time management, as is saving documents to the cloud and digital archives.

6. *Always check credit card debt.* Owning a credit card also means paying attention to fee rates as well as interest rates. Therefore, it is necessary to know how to spend the money on your card wisely so that you always maintain a positive balance from one month to the next and have an emergency fund always available.

RAISE CAPITAL TO START THE ENTERPRISE

Although the initial cost of starting a vending machine business is not particularly high, it is not certain that with only your own finances, you will be financially able to start the business.

For this, you can resort to financing after designing a business plan that considers all the expenses you will have to face in the start-up phase of the business.

Within the business plan you will have to list all the items related to the initial investment:

- The type of business you intend to start.
- The cost of the machinery or equipment to be purchased.
- The expenses related to renting the premises.
- The monthly expenses you expect to meet.

Only after considering all these elements can you submit a plan to apply for financing so that you can bring your business to life.

Here are some financing options to keep in mind when applying for a loan:

- **An Unsecured loan** refers to a loan that is provided by lenders who rely on the credit reputation of the borrower without in return any type of asset as collateral. This type of loan presents more risk to the lender and is based on very strict criteria. Examples of unsecured loans include personal loans and credit cards.

- If you want a **Short-term business loan** from a reputable lending institution, you have to be a business owner for at least 12 months. In cases of an approved loan, the applicant for such a loan will have the money in his account in a short time, to be repaid over a period typically of 18 months or less. In this situation, however, the borrower must put up an asset of his own as collateral. That asset will then revert to the lending institution if the debt is not repaid, attempting to resell it to recover the amount loaned.

- **The Equipment financing:** generally, is the largest expense to be incurred; the size of the loan in this case depends on the cost of the equipment and can also be in the form of leasing. In this way, in case of a defaulted debt, the equipment is recovered from the lender.

- **401(K) rollover** can be interesting for a vending machine owner. Some vending machine companies make available several options in agreement with the Internal Revenue Service that allow those who intend to start the business to be able to access certain funds without having to pay taxes or be penalized.

- **Home equity line of credit (HELOC)** can be your solution if you are a homeowning entrepreneur. You can use the latter as collateral by applying for a loan based on the portion of the mortgage that has already been paid off.

- **SBA LOAN:** this type of loan, despite the fact that it requires requirements to be met in order to have access to it, generally proves to be very important for those small businesses that have an impeccable credit history behind them, particularly for the purchase of equipment or provision of working capital. With this type of loan, one can apply from $500,000 to $5 million.

Of course, consulting different financial institutions, instead of relying on the first one that comes along, will help you understand which of the options you offer best match your goals and what you have in mind.

LIST OF RECOMMENDED LENDING INSTITUTIONS

Once the business plan is prepared, with all the costs and expenses related to machinery, products, utilities, and whatnot, we will have to move on in search of lenders.

Here is a list of them:

Crest Capital: this financing institution specializes in equipment loans of up to $1 million with 100 percent cost financing.

It acts very quickly in approving loans, which are granted only to companies that have been in business for at least two years and have a good credit record behind them.

National funding: this finance helps small businesses which have been operating for at least six months meet certain credit conditions.

Both new and used equipment can be purchased without down payments being required.

Currency: this institution specializes in making loans of up to $500,000 (repayable a 72 months) even in a day's time to those businesses that do not have a good credit history. They generally offer loans to all credit profiles.

Fundera: this institution allows both long-term and short-term loans, SBA loans, and several lines of credit.

It is possible to apply for up to $600,000 to invest in real estate, equipment, or as working capital, repayable in 5 to 6 years, while the lines of credit have repayments ranging from 3 to 18 months.

Lendio: Long- and short-term loans, lines of credit, and SBA loans are also available at this lending institution.

Financing is given for business start-ups, equipment purchases, and working capital. For short-term loans and lines of credit, a loan of up to $500,000 repayable over a period of one to three years is given, while for equipment purchase, one can apply for up to $5 million repayable between 1 and 5 years.

Fora financial: specializes in short-term loans ranging from $5,000 to $500,000, repayable over a 15-month period, for the purchase of equipment, inventory, and working money.

Financing is made available within 24 hours.

Credibly: Several lines of credit, short-term loans, SBA loans, and other types of financing are available at this institution.

While business expansion loans can go up to $250,000 and are repayable over a 24-month period, cash loans can go up to a sum of $400,000 and be repayable in 18 months. Financing is made available in a matter of days.

HOW TO PREPARE A LOAN APPLICATION

Once you have identified the amount of money you need for your goals, the time in which you estimate you will be able to pay it back, and the institution that best meets your needs, there will be to place alongside your business plan a loan application that is as convincing as possible.

You have to start with the fact that in order to have your proposal approved by the lending institution, it is a matter of presenting the company in a particularly positive light, explaining how and why it deserves a positive response to the loan request, and how the loan itself will be used for the start-up or development of the company, depending on the individual case.

What the institution from which the loan is applied for is particularly interested in are basically four parameters:

1. The amount of the loan you are applying for;
2. How will you use the loan;
3. How will you repay the loan;
4. How the company will operate in case of non-repayment.

In a loan proposal therefore, unlike a business plan, the focus is not on branding, or marketing, etc.. Still, the whole issue instead revolves around the budgets of the individual or company that is applying for the loan.

Although a loan proposal does not have to be as long as a business plan, the following items should still be included:

- *Executive summary* is cover letter or loan application letter in which you present your company and its background, why you need a loan, and how you plan to invest it if it is approved.
- *Brief business overview is* a section very similar to a business plan: basically, you enter a short description of the company, how it is structured, its brand, the goal you intend to achieve, the business model, the company's turnover, and the number of employees (the last two items only if you can enter them).
- In *Sales and revenue strategy* you have to describe what you are selling, thus the product with its cost and selling price, as well as the expected earnings from its sale every month.
- Lending institutions, particularly those specializing in SBA loans, have an interest in understanding how you came up with the loan amount, so you will need to submit all quotes regarding vendors, monthly budget, start-up expenses, etc in the *Loan request and use of the loan* part.
- The *Proof of repayment* part covers everything related to the loan applicant's repayment criteria, considering the amount being requested. The lending institution will want evidence about the applicant's ability to repay, such as cash flow, soundness of accounts, and sales prospects. In addition, if loan applicants are already facing another repayment, they will have to demonstrate the ability to meet the additional debt.
- *The personal and financial history of business owner is* the section regarding personal credit history, general tax

returns for the past 3 years, residential address, curriculum vitae, and how much of one's personal savings were invested in the company's establishment.

- *A copy of contractual agreements* is useful in case you have already made contracts with vendors for rent or for any other expenses, as well as permits and licenses, you should attach them to the loan proposal.

At the time of applying for a loan, it is legitimate to **expect several questions from those who borrow to finance it**, just as those who need the loan take care to rely on those who nevertheless put forward a clear proposal without hidden quibbles.

THIRTEEN
CREDIT CARD READERS FOR VENDING MACHINES

When we think of vending machines, we basically think of a stress-free "experience": you don't have to wait in line as if you were in a store, for example. Unless they are poorly maintained, the vending machines are always well stocked, and therefore we are likely to see what we need at that moment, be it a snack, a drink, or anything else related to the need of the moment.

An element of annoyance could be the machine that gets stuck, or that eats the money without giving what you intended to buy. There is usually always a telephone number to contact for cases like this.

To get around this type of problem, it is becoming increasingly common to install machines where it is possible to pay with a credit card instead of cash.

This type of solution, which can be found installed on the latest generation of vending machines, in which there are special chips, has advantages for both consumers and owners of vending machines: consumers do not risk having their cash locked in a machine, as well as being able to keep track of their purchases, owners because they can better control based on sales when it is time to replenish their machines.

Using vending machines with credit cards allows consumers to buy many more products at once, without considering the limit that one would have with cash. And of course that means more sales for the operator more revenue.

At the same time, this allows for far more efficient management of time and money; in fact, there are several apps or at any rate technologies that allow for remote vending machine management, eliminating all the manual data entry part as well as giving real-time news on sales trends and product inventory.

When deciding to make use of machines capable of reading a credit card, a vending machine owner must keep in mind as a basic principle that they must be easy to use and somehow must instill in the user a sense of security. They must also be able to accept credit cards as well as debit cards, and be convenient to use.

In short, they must be secure, easy to use, and compatible with different types of cards.

Here are some suggestions on what are considered among the best credit card readers for vending machines:

1. Cantaloupe ePort

With Cantaloupe Eport, you can accept all types of payments with different methods and different devices.

Whether you sell products or services or pay by credit or debit card, you can accept payments anywhere.

USA Technologies, a leader in wireless technology and online payments and services, owns this technology.

Take a look at the website to learn about its products.

[Image: QR-code.png]

Its Eport package includes a card reader and telemetry system capable of reading different types of cards, as well as being able to support different payment modes.

It features a sleek design and can read magnetic stripe devices and supporting NFC technology.

Regarding costs, USA Technologies talks about a fixed monthly fee and a percentage based on average sales. The fixed monthly payment is $7.95, while the commission costs are 5.95 percent of the transition.

2. Airvend/365 Retail

Airvend is a multifunctional interactive tablet: not only does it provide information about the nutritional values of products that are in vending machines, but it also allows you to pay as you prefer, magnetic stripe cards, for example, but also via mobile wallet.

Arvind was founded in 2012, immediately distinguishing itself as a manufacturer of electronic components and computers. 365 Retails Market later acquired it.

The fee that is charged monthly is $15 per device, while the percentage on commissions is around 5 percent.

. . .

3. PicoVend Mini

PicoVend mini is a small vending machine with a compact size, making it ideal for adapting to different machine models.

PicoVend Mini relies on the 365 PicoPlatform, which provides a whole range of tools, services and products for vending machines.

You can use this platform to improve your machines, making them more efficient. It uses touchless technology, and the fact that the nutritional values of the various food products sold can be read on the screen can make the user experience more personalized and convenient.

Ultimately, the PicoVend mini is ideal for those who want to offer a pleasant and convenient experience. For example, it is possible to pay with ET&T SIM cards.

4. 365 Touchless Vending

This is an innovative solution, because it can be used simply through a Bluetooth connection. This eliminates any problems regarding setting up a connection between vending machines and smartphones.

5. Nayax VPOS Touch Cashless Credit Card Reader

Since 2005, Nayax has been a leader in providing a whole range of solutions and services for the vending machine industry, so much so that it has 200,000 of its own vending machines scattered around the world.

VPOS proves to be a secure and reliable payment solution that can read both chip and magnetic stripe cards. Interaction with the consumer can also take place through voice. This solution is compatible with virtually all types of vending machines.

The payment options offered by Nayax without resorting to cash are many, such as debit cards, credit cards, e-commerce, bank accounts, etc.

Added to this is the speed of the transaction, in the sense that there are not many steps to perform, such as connecting to a merchant account and initiating a connexion to a payment gateway. There is also the ability to offer discounts and propose various offers.

Increase your revenue by 30% & Cut Your Cost Down by 20%

According to experts, this type of platform can increase sales by up to 30 percent.

This is also thanks to a number of solutions that promote their vending machines through various channels, as well as provide you with information on sales made.

To an increase in offers, we also have a lowering of operating costs of around 20 percentage points.

All this is possible thanks to the possibility offered to manage all your business online, so you only need to have a device that has access to the network. In this way, the costs of keeping the business up and running tend to go down.

Another strength of Nayax is its customer service, which is very efficient.

In fact, in case of problems or any request, there is a very specific representative to whom one can refer, who is professionally well trained and able to deal with any kind of question.

Question: Do I Need a Chip-Enabled Card to Use a Vending Machine?

Although banks are increasingly favoring chip cards over magnetic stripe cards, ATMs are still set up for this type of card, so there is no problem using it to pay for purchased items.

The process that takes place is basically the same as when you store in the store: you insert the card into the reader, which then communicates with your bank asking you to remove it, once the transaction is complete.

Recall also how all chip-equipped cards also have an integrated magnetic stripe.

This means that in case the transaction is not accepted and therefore, you cannot proceed with the purchase, the machine is waiting for you to swipe the card.

Is the Vending Machine Credit Card Reader Secure?

The answer to this question is yes, the credit card readers we find at ATMs are secure; they are designed to be secure.

In fact, when the card is inserted into the slot, it is encrypted, a process that remains in place until you decide what to pay for. Then, each time a purchase is made, the data code changes accordingly. This is the main reason why chip technology manages to be so resistant to various frauds.

When you enter the transaction code, it is sent to your bank, which in turn transfers it to the receiving bank. In this case, as would be the case with credit cards, the ATM does not require any signature or PIN code.

One advantage of chip cards over magnetic stripe cards is the shorter transaction processing time. In fact, the data are transferred in real-time, allowing the various payment steps to be managed and monitored live.

FOURTEEN
THE MINDSET FOR A SUCCESSFUL BUSINESS

In this bonus chapter, we will devote time to one particular element, not explicitly related to the vending machine business, but fundamental to starting any kind of business: we are talking about the mindset.

Having the right mindset is crucial: when things seem not to go as planned, not giving up in the face of difficulties but rather looking for the silver lining is a key element that distinguishes a successful business from a failing one.

It's not just about coping with the different obstacles. It's about having the right enthusiasm, the right attitude, the right charisma to create your own business and make it successful.

Everyone has a different view of success: for some people saving enough to buy their dream car may be an achievement to celebrate. For others it might be being able to buy a house to live in with the person they love and for still others making income from a passive income each month.

The success we are looking for in our case is linked to the vending machine business, to its success, to whether we will be able to achieve that coveted economic independence that the growth of our vending machines will ensure.

The key element in being able to manage the emotional challenges involved in creating and running a business is to be able to reprogram one's mind.

The first step in embarking on this path of awareness is to never think that being successful is more a matter of luck than anything else, but to understand that, as much as a dash of good fortune is welcome, it will be a good strategy, the right approach and a positive mindset that will bring success to your business.

Reorganizing your mind is not as difficult as it may seem: it is not so much essential to think positively as it is to change your thinking patterns, training your mind to always look for a path to success in any situation, even the most desperate one.

This skill is called problem-solving, and it is essential when, while running a business, a problem of any kind should burden you. It will be up to you to decide how to handle the situation, deciding whether the problem will be a setback to your earnings or whether there is a solution that will allow you to continue your business, perhaps compromising but avoiding losing valuable earnings.

Understand your mind

It may not be your case, but it is very common for the subconscious mind to develop mechanics capable of anchoring you in preconceptions and ideas that do not allow you to achieve the goals you set for yourself.

This happens because each of us has a history behind us made up of both positive and negative events, which unconsciously program our subconscious and make us think and perform actions completely automatically.

It is exactly like driving a car: once we learn the functions of the pedals, we do not need to constantly think about which one to press in the moment of need, we will do it automatically and without thinking about it for a second. The same happens with the thoughts and habits that inhabit our subconscious: if we have told ourselves too many times that investing money in a business is too risky for our pockets or that no one will want to buy from our vending machines, we will start off on the wrong foot and not steer the business in the right direction.

Success works exactly like this: when we visualize in our minds the outcome of our efforts to create a business, we must imagine it being successful. Therefore, working with an image of success in mind, when accompanied by positive actions and awareness, can really make a difference, but in order to function it is crucial not to have a generic image of success in mind.

Set yourself a realistic and achievable goal, and commit yourself to get there with your abilities: in your case, it could be to start earning your first $300 monthly passive dollars, a figure not too high but still better than 0. This figure, being plausible, can actually be achieved, leading your subconscious to feel a sense of satisfaction once you achieve it.

Thereafter, you can set new goals in your mind so that you have a constant challenge to overcome and a series of rewards that will allow you to receive a boost of positivity every time you achieve them.

Repeat your goals

Your mind does not work like a computer: once you set a goal, it will not be in your thoughts all the time; in fact, over the course of months, while you are busy creating the business and moving it forward, it will be very easy to forget about it.

This is why a technique widely used by successful entrepreneurs is to write down your goals on paper every night before you go to bed or in the morning once you wake up, so that you can keep your focus on your priorities.

Doing this prepares your mind to make decisions designed to move you in specific directions in a completely subconscious way, creating a constant reminder of what you really need to get to the finish line of your goal.

Writing down your goals and placing them in a prominent place, such as your home refrigerator or the background of your smartphone, can be a great way to continue to stay focused.

. . .

Be specific

When you write your goal, don't do it in a general way: if you want to start a vending machine business, write down exactly the elements that your business will not be able to lack.

For example, you might write that your business will be placed in a room of at least 20 square meters, with at least three tables and chairs to allow your customers to consume, with two vending machines for edibles and one for drinks. Beyond that, write down who you want your vendors to be and how your business will be assorted. Imagine the color of the walls and furniture, the type of music you want inside, and any other elements.

Having specific and precise visual ideas about your actions can make a difference, positively influencing your subconscious mind.

Don't stop reprogramming your mind.

Depending on your background, you have been thinking a certain way for years and acting accordingly.

When you try to change your mindset, but find yourself thinking the way you used to, don't give up: it is perfectly normal to remain bound to a way of thinking that you have adopted all your life, because your mind has been trained to believe in a certain way.

It's like a 120-pound bodybuilder who decides to become a marathon runner: his weight won't allow him to run 50 kilometers the first time he decides to train, but if he trains persistently, he might be able to readjust his heavy body for a different sport.

Do not underestimate the power of instant and short-term gratification. As mentioned earlier, setting attainable and scalable goals is the secret to getting far: a bodybuilder might decide to lose a pound a month before becoming a marathon runner, because a distant goal like running 50 kilometers can weigh on the mind by being perpetually unattainable and leading more simply to giving up.

Think about it, what is easier, climbing 100 steps or overcoming a five-meter wall?

Set time limits

Deciding to get to a finish line in a short period of time is not always the right choice: You may even have the resources to get it done, but if it causes you so much stress that you can't handle the workload and arrive at the finish line completely exhausted, you won't have the energy to pursue the next steps to start the business.

Stress can lead you to make rash decisions, damaging your mental well-being. That's why I advise you to consider extra time when you give yourself a deadline so that you can fit perfectly into the time frame and not arrive at the deadline having to put in maximum effort.

However, it is also true that some people benefit from time limits because of the adrenaline rush that having to meet a deadline can give. If you are this type of person, you can give yourself tighter deadlines to motivate you to do better, but always with the knowledge that you can miss them and still be on time.

Setbacks and failures

Many face a setback or failure of an idea that one was pursuing with passion and spending precious resources.

This, too, is part of the road to success, as long as you do not view the failure or setback as a stopping point, but a new starting point.

Learn from the mistake

Learning from mistakes is crucial for a great entrepreneur: a mistake is nothing more than an attempt made gone wrong, and one that you know you should never make again if you want to pursue a business.

Sooner or later, everyone makes a mistake, however much the

impact of one mistake may not be the same as another, but it is up to us to decide how we view the mistake.

Refrain from letting the mistake drive your decisions by stopping you from doing business, but use it as a lesson to do better, differently, and more effectively.

Back on the right track

How satisfying is it to succeed despite adversity? A mistake can be the best incentive to do better, because when you succeed in achieving your goals despite the challenge you faced and the mistake you made, you will feel an even greater sense of satisfaction. This self-confidence will be the best fuel for moving your business forward.

Accept the emotions

A mistake, failure, or setback can take a toll on the psyche of entrepreneurs, leading them to experience a range of negative emotions.

When this happens, it may be a good idea to stop for a while by forgoing gains in favor of your mental health. Taking time to understand how you feel and where you went wrong can make all the difference, getting you off to a fresh start aware of your abilities, mistakes, and actions you need to take to get your business back on track.

Don't give up

Successful people who succeeded in reaching their goals faced so many difficulties and found solutions, having to readjust their business according to market needs, studying them, understanding them, and making compromises. Giving up was never an option for them, so they worked to change the state of affairs.

If your business turns out differently than you hope, don't let it get you down: analyze your mistakes, take a break, and come back to try again in a new way and with a well-thought-out plan.

· · ·

Look at things in perspective

It happens to many entrepreneurs that they stop just at the moment when the finish line is very close, because you are not looking at your business from another point of view: ask yourself where you started and how far you have come, so you can realize how far you really are from your goal. This exercise could put everything in a new perspective.

Change your priorities

When starting a business, it may not be obvious to everyone that you are starting something very complex. Give yourself a goal and help those around you understand that you are not playing games, and that you will need time to take care of the details of your new business.

This time will be taken away from personal affections, hobbies, and pleasures. So make sure you also have support from the circle of people you hold closest.

When you get to the goal, don't stop

Many people believe that getting it right is the end of the line, but a successful entrepreneur knows there is nothing worse than stopping: always find new stimulation, set new goals and start working again to reach your goal. Every house is built by placing brick upon brick.

Don't stop learning

Whatever your earnings, never stop allocating a portion of your budget to training: there is always something new to learn, and there is no right time to stop studying.

Remember: there is no better satisfaction than finding the solution to a problem instantly through your prior knowledge, obtainable through both field experience and study.

. . .

Always Do Networking

A key element of any borrower's success, having access to a reliable network of professionals who can help you achieve your goals will not only allow you faster financial growth, but also faster personal growth.

Being inspired by people who get up in the morning every day, like you, knowing they have to run a business with all its satisfactions and problems, can inspire you to do better, point you to quick and effective solutions to problems we are facing, and create partnerships with someone you can really trust.

Healthy mind in healthy body

It may seem like an add-on to some, but being well in your body is crucial to allowing your mind to function at 100 percent.

When we consume high-fat or high-sugar foods too often, we make our bodies less efficient, affecting the speed and clarity of the mind's functioning.

Following a healthy diet, indulging in treats from time to time, and exercising can really help you with your productivity and the quality of the choices you make throughout the day.

Maintain an efficient sleep rhythm

Getting little sleep is not good for your mind, and keeping late hours to sleep during daylight hours will take time away from your business.

Waking up early is the habit shared by so many successful people, who choose the early hours of the morning to work in complete peace of mind, while also finding time during the day to exercise.

Getting enough sleep will keep your mind clear and ready to make the best decisions for your business.

Keep toxic people out of your life

The relationships you choose to pursue can make a real difference when everything goes wrong: If your business was failing, who would you rather have by your side? A person who keeps telling you you're not going to make it, or someone who can motivate you to get back on track?

Negative people tend to belittle your plans, saying phrases like "you can't do it," "it's too complicated," "it takes too much effort." These people will lower the chances that you will succeed in your venture before you even start working on it.

Surround yourself with people who know how to encourage you, love you and want the best for your life, and help you in the endeavor.

Keep alcohol and drugs away

It's not always the people around you who are the biggest obstacle to reaching your goal-sometimes we ourselves are our own biggest anchor, due to toxic addictions that take up time, make us sick, and focus our mental energies on something that will never lead to anything good.

If you really want to start a successful business to change your life, choose to reduce to the point of eliminating substance use, and find new priorities for your life.

Be grateful

When all seems not to be going well, and negativity takes over, look back at all that you have struggled to achieve: the early gains generated by your vending machines, though still few, are still better than zero, that is, the passive gains you were able to make before you started a business!

If you made it this far, you were still stronger than so many other people out there who never made it to the same milestone as you.

Give yourself a reward

What could be better after working hard, spending your time constructively, and getting fantastic results than rewarding yourself?

There are many kinds of rewards, choose them according to your preferences: if you are among those who love fashion, treat yourself to a new dress. If you love to travel, plan a trip somewhere. If you love sweets and are on a diet, treat yourself to a snack now and then.

FIFTEEN
AN ECOFRIENDLY BUSINESS

The environment is an issue that is truly close to the hearts of many business owners and consumers around the world.

Deciding to adopt new and, above all, environmentally friendly methods would make you not only mindful of the needs of the planet, but also the first choice for customers who most want to respect the environment.

What is an eco-friendly vending machine?

Eco-friendly vending machines are Energy Star rated, and use as much as 40% less energy than ordinary vending machines. This not only translates into helping the environment, but also saving money on your utility bills!

If a machine is Energy Star rated, then you know it is environmentally friendly.

One of the elements that best protects the environment is The natural refrigerant that has been applied by the Coca brand, which can replace the harmful greenhouse gas HFC.

If you have a vending machine built before this refrigerant was used, contact the manufacturer and ask for a replacement.

One item that consumes electricity, proving to be an unnecessary waste of energy, is lighting.

When your room is empty, there will be no one to turn off the lights, resulting in energy waste that can be easily eliminated. One solution is to use motion-sensing equipment that can automatically turn lights off and on without wasting electricity.

The bulbs themselves are one element that can make the business spend more money: fluorescent bulbs greatly increase costs, while LED or CFL bulbs have really low power consumption, as well as a long lifespan.

Total electricity savings with these types of bulbs are around 65 percent, and on average they can last over 50000 hours.

Another method of saving money is to control the activity of the vending machine: just as with room lights, you can turn off the lights inside the machine when it has not been used for some time.

The solution that best respects the environment and will save you 100 percent of the money is definitely not to turn on the lights in the vending machine at all: a sign indicating that the machines are running will suffice.

If your budget allows, it will be possible to install solar panels that can power the vending machines, creating true eco-friendly refrigeration.

The products you put in the vending machines should also be environmentally friendly: this is the case with SPE certifications, which are awarded to products that are free of environmentally harmful packaging, produced organically and in an environmentally friendly manner.

Another way to help the environment is to allow your customers to drink without necessarily having to buy bottled water: there are water dispensers that sell water at a modest price, preventing the customer from producing trash.

These dispensers work the same way for the sugary drinks we are all familiar with.

This way, by bringing a bottle from home, customers can drink without producing trash!

Finally, as is the case in many American cities and northern European countries, recycling machines are a great idea to help the environment through vending machines: you can get money by inserting plastic, glass or aluminum bottles into the machine, selling rewarded for recycling. In addition, it is an initiative that helps keep the city clean, thanks to the contribution of those who are less fortunate and don't have jobs, who dedicate themselves to collecting recyclable bottles to scrape together money.

If you are thinking of starting a green initiative with your new vending machine business, either because you love the environment or to attract customers who care about it, then follow the tips listed in this chapter.

SIXTEEN

FAQS

We have analyzed as broadly and exhaustively as possible everything revolving around the vending machine business, its costs, the time and money needed to start the business, how to protect yourself and how to apply for loans.

In case you still have doubts, we include below the most frequently asked questions to dispel all your doubts.

How can I create a service that is the best possible for my clients?

Consider the key element in this type of business: there is no direct contact with customers. So to make the service as good as possible, the advice is to make the shopping experience great, for example, by researching what customers like best. Regularly restocking your distributor is also a good strategy to make customers happy. If you also can, use integrated distributors with the latest technology.

What is the product mix?

It is a matter of figuring out what kind of customers might choose you to buy something to eat or drink and figuring out what kind of product or products customers will buy after they have already taken another one. For example, after taking a package of chips, they are likely to want to drink something to quench their thirst. Or, again, if your typical customer is a fitness enthusiast, they will be looking for a diet product and, consequently, a low-calorie drink.

It is up to you to figure out what types of products to provide to the public with your vending machines.

How much time will I have to devote every month to my vending machine business?

In that case, it is difficult to indicate the time you will have to spend on your business. There are several variants to consider: picking up products from suppliers, putting them inside the machine, recovering the money earned, add to that the time spent on breakdowns, scheduling repairs, etc.

One tip is to automate some steps, such as inventory management and payment collection.

With relatively low initial costs, is the vending machine business profitable?

Several factors are also to be considered here, such as location, product novelty and price, target audience, and brand awareness.

We also consider expenses for maintenance and possible breakdowns.

At the end of this, we consider how one machine can earn a few dozen dollars and another several hundred within a week.

How to minimize repair and maintenance costs?

To minimize costs for repairs and maintenance, it is best to invest in a fully functional vending machine that can operate for 24 hours a day with minimal service.

When purchasing a vending machine, rely on a company with a good reputation and excellent customer service.

In addition, buying a reconditioned vending machine could save you the repair costs of a used machine.

How often should I refill my vending machine?

You must monitor sales volumes to determine how often to restock your distributors. Remember that the more a product sells, the more frequently you will have to restock the distributor. Of course, we are not talking about restocking all products every time, but only those that are most sold.

Is there a need to wash the vending machines?

Yes, especially when selling food products. The inside of vending machines require less frequent cleaning since they are not in contact with the outside, compared to the outside parts such as the glass or the keypad. In fact, the latter requires more cleaning.

Warm water, a detergent sponge, and a towel are sufficient for cleaning.

Place a disinfectant gel inside the vending machine area so patrons can sanitize their machines before using the keypad, and ensure the gel is always in the machine.

. . .

What percentage of earnings do I have to pay to the owner of the site where I set up the vending machines?

Generally, you have to agree on the amount to pay from the start. This commission is based on net sales and can be as high as 20 percent of those sales.

Of course, it is always possible to negotiate and come to a different agreement.

Who should I turn to for vending machine maintenance?

Several mechanical and electronic parts make up a vending machine. Therefore, it is usually a good idea to call in a worker who specializes in repairing vending machines.

In case of a malfunction, the technician might go to the site and then draw up an estimate.

If a part is found to be malfunctioning, its cost is not included in the technician's call-out and labor rate.

What is the ideal business structure for a vending company?

To begin with, the one that provides the best benefits is the formation of an LLC corporation since it involves a lot of tax aid, protects against the risks associated with the business, and gives credibility to the company. Nothing, however, prevents you from changing the company's structure once earnings begin to increase and you want to expand your business.

Can I install my vending machines anywhere?

Before installing your vending machines, you must consult the local laws and contact the owners of the place you have chosen, whether a person, local authority or government agency. It would be best if you also considered a whole range of recommendations and restrictions when deciding to install vending machines on school grounds or in places such as hospitals, often relating to alcohol and tobacco-containing items.

How quickly after purchasing vending machines are they installed?

It depends on several factors, usually, 15-20 days pass between purchase and installation.

If you buy a custom one, you will have to discuss the details with a representative of the company you approached, and of course, allow time to modify the device(s).

For a standard vending machine, which electrical outlet is recommended?

A 3-pin socket is required for the machine to operate, and the socket should be on in a separate circuit. It is always good to check these details to avoid problems later.

A standard vending machine needs 115 volts, at 10-12 amps, to operate.

How much does a vending machine license cost?

The price varies from state to state. We are talking about between $10 and $250.

It is always good to consult local laws and authorities before starting any business. Even in some states, there is a course on how to prepare and process food in order to obtain a license.

How can I do branding and marketing for my vending machine?

There are various possibilities for making your brand recognizable: for example, lining your vending machines with your company's logo, custom colors, and symbols. You could also include a brief history of your brand.

As far as marketing is concerned, you can create special offers, promotions, and themed discounts, creating a loyalty relationship.

As a final piece of advice, it is always a good idea, whenever possible, to enlist the help of employees, help, and support to make your business run at its best.

YOU HAVE REACHED THE END OF THIS BOOK!

I hope you enjoyed it as much as I enjoyed writing it.

I would love it if you would share your opinion with others
leaving a review!

Every single review is very important to me, because they allow me to
**find out what's missing in my book, updating it for my reader
and continue my writing activity.**

*Thank you and wish you all the luck with your vending machine
business!*

Printed in the USA
CPSIA information can be obtained
at www.ICGtesting.com
LVHW040111270124
769484LV00017B/1043